Rewire for success™

An easy guide for using neuroscience to improve choices for work, life and well-being

Vannessa McCamley

Contact Details

Vannessa McCamley

M: +61 416 148 338 | **E:** vannessa@linksuccess.com.au

Author: Vannessa McCamley

Title: Rewire for Success

An easy guide for using neuroscience to improve choices for work, life and well-being.

Publisher: linksuccess

www.linksuccess.com.au

ISBN: 978-0-6452032-0-2

First published September 2021

Copyright © Vannessa McCamley 2021

The moral right of the author has been asserted. All rights reserved. No part of this book may be reproduced or transmitted in any form or by any means, electronic or mechanical, including photocopying, recording, photography or by any information storage and retrieval system, without prior permission in writing from the publisher.

Rewire for Success™, The F.O.O.D Framework™ and The D.R.I.V.E Model™ are all considered to be trademarks of Vannessa McCamley. All rights reserved.

Dedication

To my father, Neil McCamley for always inspiring me to think big and for your guidance in turning them into a reality. Dad supported my many book ideas, and his encouragement means more to me than he will ever know. He is a humble man, rich of life and love for his family, always curious about how to live your best life. His amazing health in his 80's is a great testament to his positive mindset over the years. Thank you Dad for your inspiration, you are pure sunshine in every way, and we could all learn from the way you have lived your best life.

Thank You

To the many amazing and talented experts involved with helping me create a quality book including;

Editor – Clare Loewenthal

Reviewer and educational advisor – Deborah Palmer

Neuroscientist reviewer – Dr Delia McCabe

Graphic designer – Karina Gomez

Illustrator – Debbie Wood

Book industry consultant – Carol Nassif

Writing advisor and mentor – Chris Barclay.

Many thanks to my family and friends for your support.

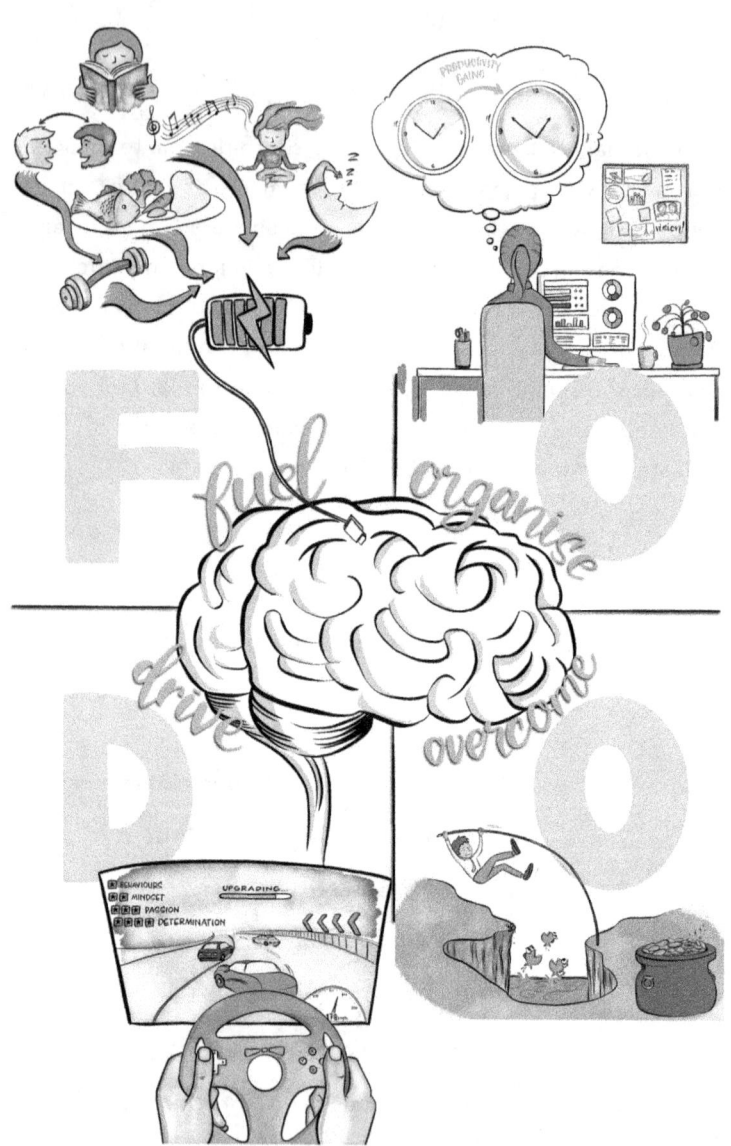

Contents

Introduction 7

How the Brain Works? 21

Section 1 43
The F.O.O.D framework overview
Fuel your brain with the right ingredients

Section 2 101
Organise your daily structure based
on when you do your best thinking

Section 3 115
Overcome obstacles with
the brain in mind

Section 4 135
Drive the right behaviours,
mindset and passion for achieving
your desired outcomes

Conclusion 159

References and resources 163

Introduction

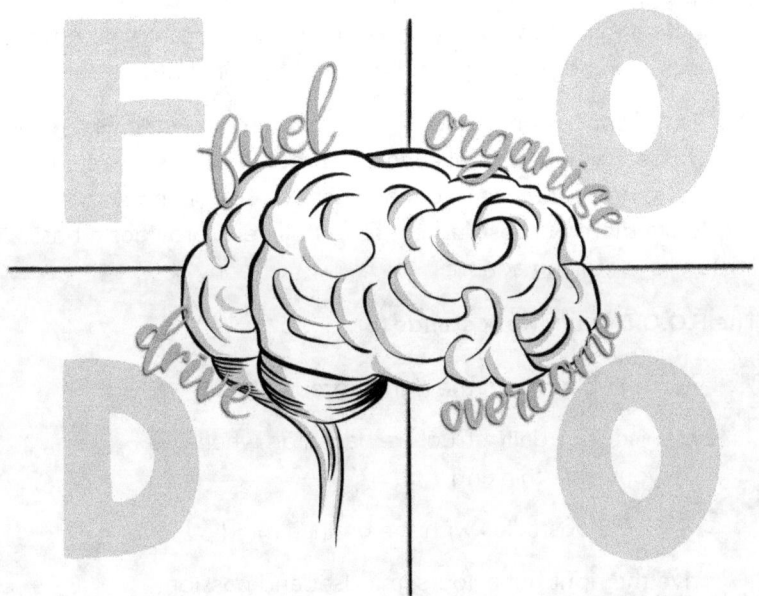

Introduction

Every day, I use one of the most fascinating and complex branches of medical science – neuroscience – to help people overcome personal and professional obstacles. Understanding how the brain works allows people to reconnect with their behavioural drivers and reminds them of the power of empathy and deep thinking. This helps them build the adaptability and resilience needed to cope with today's relentless speed of change, amid the obstacles posed by an uncertain world.

My specialties are the neuroscience of self-leadership, leading others, change readiness, peak performance, emotion regulation and renewal; skills that build resilience for successful outcomes.

I have written *Rewire for Success* to bridge the gap between what science has recently learned about how the brain operates, and people's behaviour. It's a guide to getting the most from your brain in terms of decision making, problem-solving, flexibility and innovation, by understanding how to create new connections and pathways in the brain through neuroplasticity.

Rewire for Success introduces the F.O.O.D framework, which I've created to help you take what neuroscience has revealed about the brain and use it to make behavioural changes that will result in a more purposeful, less stressful life. It provides a basic structure for taking action.

The F.O.O.D framework stands for:

F uel your brain with the right ingredients

O rganise your daily structure based on when you do your best thinking

O vercome obstacles with the brain in mind

D rive the right behaviours, mindset and passion for achieving your desired outcomes.

The F.O.O.D framework is outlined in detail in section 1.

This book is much more than one model. Because self-discovery is one of my guiding passions and values, I've explored many behavioural frameworks that have helped me face challenges over the years. Knowing what busy lives we all lead; *Rewire for Success* introduces these frameworks and provides examples of how I've seen them applied to real-life scenarios. No need to wade your way through multiple books – it's all here in one convenient resource. The book also has contributions from a range of experts I respect and trust; some I work with and some have helped me with my own personal development and growth.

Rewire for Success has been designed so it can be read in its entirety, or you can select the self-contained sections most relevant to you. Some topics may resonate with you now; some may become relevant in the future.

Because I've chosen the acronym F.O.O.D – and because we all love to eat – I use food analogies throughout the book. Here is the first: consider *Rewire for Success* to be a buffet. Select the dishes – subjects – most appealing to you and taste them.

I suggest that you pick between one and three areas that you want to focus on in the next 90 days. Once you identify the new habits, skills, or behaviours, you will learn how to integrate them into your life over the next 90 days.

Why 90 days? In my experience helping a wide range of clients, it takes approximately 90 days to create new wiring through neuroplasticity. The brain will find any more than three focus areas in 90 days too much to process and will give up or procrastinate.

After 90 days it is likely to take you less effort and energy as it becomes an automatic habit (also known as a short cut within the brain, i.e. like learning to drive a car over a period of time).

Depending on your approach, you can select one to three areas from each section or from the whole book. Alternatively, you can write down a list of actions and you prioritise them into 90 day chunks.

Your task is to evaluate what you are going to STOP doing, START doing and CONTINUE doing. You may discover that some of these brain-friendly strategies are already a part of your routine, which should give you confidence and allow you to focus on other areas of your life.

Neuroscience is complex, so I've provided examples of how the biological processes influence human behaviour to make the scientific explanations more digestible. Sometimes the case studies are clients I have worked with, and often they are drawn from my own life. I have included my stories to demonstrate that despite my expertise in neuroscience, I too have flaws and obstacles and goals yet to reach, a life of possibilities and obstacles to overcome.

What is neuroscience?

Neuroscience explains human behaviour in terms of brain activity; how the brain marshals its billions of individual nerve cells to produce behaviour, and how the environment influences these cells.

In recent years, we have learnt more about the brain due to technology advances such as functional magnetic resonance imaging (fMRI), which tracks blood flow and electroencephalogram scans (EEG). An EEG is a test that tracks and records brain wave patterns, and identifies problems related to electrical activity in the brain.

Often our brains are on autopilot, and we have little understanding of how our biggest asset works. Neuroscience shows us better ways to think, problem-solve, make decisions and innovate. Understanding neuroscience allows us to tap into the brain's capacity for extraordinary experiences and learn how to get 'unstuck' from day-to-day obstacles and challenges.

Why neuroscience: Why now?

Why is it the perfect time to embrace neuroscience? Because at no time in history have individuals been expected to cope with so much change or absorb and act on so much information, across so many communication channels. The expectation that we must function faster impacts on the way we live, and on our physical and mental health.

We are at a tipping point: individuals are burning out with huge to-do lists, overwhelmed by urgent deadlines that eat away at critical thinking, imagination, judgement, and mental and physical health. Ultimately, this also damages families, communities, business, and government. The next few years will see the speed of change increase, primarily due to technological advances in the workplace. This, too, will affect people's mental health.

These systemic dysfunctions were emphasised when the COVID-19 pandemic struck. Suddenly, individuals lost the personal freedom they had taken for granted. Around the world people were left to work out what the new normal looked like for themselves and others. Uncertainty and change came into focus.

However, amidst all this turmoil, the art of imagination is back. Over the past decade, we have placed an incredibly high value on immediacy and execution, wringing deep thinking and creativity out of many parts of our professional lives. But the tide is turning. As we head into a future where machines, and artificial intelligence (AI), take care of menial work, there will be a greater premium on creativity. Now is the time to learn how to harness the power of neuroscience, to create more ways, and better ways to gain perspective. Now is the time to rewire our brains to ensure we give the machines plenty of effective direction.

My personal story of overcoming obstacles and finding purpose

A bit about my beloved Dad: I'm the youngest of four children, and Dad has always been a rock for my family and me. As a teenager, my friends had heroes plastered on their walls, but Dad was my hero. He is now in his 80s and still glistening with life, always curious about the world around him. He has been happy 99 per cent of his life; always looking at the bright side, always seeing an obstacle as an opportunity.

1992 - So, picture me: I'm 16 years of age, sitting with Dad on the back veranda in the sun. I'm pondering what I'm going to do when I finish high school and worrying about my future direction. I'm a student who has given her best but struggled to get the outstanding results I aimed for. I'm an average scholar with driving ambition.

"Dad, what's the special skill or talent I have that's going to allow me to set the world on fire and make a significant difference?" I ask.

He looks up at the universe, ponders my question, stares into my eyes and gleefully responds, *"Your gift is people."*

Feeling happy by his profound response, but also a little confused, I reply, *"What the heck (swearing wasn't an option) does 'people' mean Dad'?"*

"Since you were young, you've always been able to connect with all types of people with compassion and acceptance. You've guided them through their problems and helped them to explore possible options and opportunities. Not just with your friends but their parents, actually with anyone who came across your path, needing a hand".

I think to myself, *"Oh no, Dad is losing the plot and talking in riddles again."*

Dad was right, though. Recently I reflected on my career journey, which began with retail sales, before moving to hospitality jobs in hotels and the Sydney Casino high roller's room. I've had marketing and sales roles within leading IT companies that led me to manage and lead people for the Asia Pacific region and around the world. Today, I run my own leadership and performance consulting business. The common thread in all these career changes and study is **'PEOPLE'**.

Despite my success, I have spent my working life searching for my true purpose and destiny. I grew up on fairy tales and stories with happy endings, and it always felt like if I could only achieve my next goal or milestone, I would be happy. But at each turning point, there was another mountain to climb, a harder, bigger mountain that took more energy. I was an opportunist, and in my 20s, I had loads of energy and was driven to make a difference in the corporate world. I took every opportunity to make new connections, as I flew around the world, adding value.

Today my work makes a significant difference in the lives of others, and I am becoming more open in trusting life's uncertainty, surrendering to future possibilities, letting go of the expectations of other people and applying key learnings to life's challenges.

Let me share some of the major obstacles that changed my journey and helped steer my course to you through this book

By the time I am 26-years old (2002), I have changed my career twice and switched my studies from hospitality and business management to marketing management. I have a job managing and leading people around Asia Pacific that requires me to be on planes every two to three weeks and contributing to my employer's double-digit growth year on year. I am working an average of 80 hours a week and living on a diet of stress and immediacy. Work has become my focus.

Abruptly, I hit a speed bump on my 'road to greatness' when I get sick with the early stages of cervical cancer. Thinking that I'm way too young and healthy to be ill, I see health only in terms of fitness and eating well. My attitude is, 'It will be okay. I'll have the operation and be back at work pronto.' I do not want to miss a beat at work because there are key performance indicators (KPIs) to achieve, bonuses to earn and shares to acquire. I am still striving to be on the top of the performance bell curve.

I enter a hospital for cervical cancer surgery, which ends up being more complicated than expected. This leaves me with a question mark over whether I will be able to have children in the future. After the operation, every joint in my entire body swells up, and I cannot walk to the bathroom unassisted. My boyfriend carries me around for almost a month. I visit various doctors and have numerous tests to find the source of my pain. When the medical world can't provide answers, I turn to natural therapies.

I see a top naturopath and change my diet, which I only stick to until my body bounces back to normal. Amidst all this, I lie in bed and work like crazy on my laptop to ensure that work projects progress. My mindset does not change. I'm a junkie, addicted to stress and achieving business goals. I'm a crazy perfectionist who thinks working harder and longer will always produce the desired results. Little do I know what lies ahead of me.

New Orleans: A turning point

2003 – I am a Marketing Manager for Microsoft, and along with 13,000 team members from all over the world, I am travelling to the company's annual sales kick-off events in New Orleans. This event takes place two years before Cyclone Katrina erupts and destroys much of the city's interesting history. I am lucky to experience this spiritual place before the destruction.

My mentor and colleague from our New Zealand office, Mansur Zwart, who has been with Microsoft for years and visited New Orleans many times, arranges a tour for us before the event. We travel around on Harley Davidson bikes on the opposite side of the road to Australia. We visit amazing plantations that are like something out of the movies, eat yummy creole seafood on the side streets of the Mississippi River and visit the French Quarter. It is an unforgettable day as I experience the city's freedom. Yet I also feel sadness for New Orleans' cruel history of slavery.

Two months after this amazing trip, I marry and fall pregnant soon after. My mentor Mansur announces he has a rare type of cancer. Once I recover from the shock of his announcement, I decide that if anyone can beat this, it's Mansur. He has one of the most remarkable mindsets for overcoming obstacles I have observed.

I return from maternity leave to learn that Mansur has passed away. I cannot describe how devasted I am in this moment of grief. I think about how Mansur was only 45 years of age and had such a zest for life. I think about how he has left behind his loving partner and his girls whom he adored. I describe Mansur as a modern-day James Dean (an American actor from the '50s) who lived life to the fullest. Mansur loved riding his Harley Davison motorbike in his full leathers. It gave him a sense of freedom to have the wind in his face, and it sure was fun riding alongside the Mississippi River together. Thank goodness he was a good rider because our adventure was only a couple of months before my marriage and I told him I had to make my wedding day in one piece, which I did!

At the same time that I'm experiencing all this sadness, after multiple miscarriages and against the odds, I finally give birth to my amazing son, Caleb.

A working mother with a sick child

2005 – I am the primary income earner when I return to work after my maternity leave, and it is a challenge to have a child who develops severe asthma at three months of age. I have lost my mate and mentor, Mansur, and I'm trying to find a new rhythm that allows me to get work done when I'm only getting a few hours' sleep per night. I am stressed out of my brain, to be brutally honest. I have no family support nearby and sleep deprivation leaves my marriage on tender hooks.

In 2006, Caleb's lung collapses when he is 18 months old, and he starts to turn blue. My local doctor tells me to rush him to emergency as an ambulance won't make it in time. The car ride is the most stressful situation of my life, my baby gasping for air in the baby seat as I weave amongst traffic. His vital signs are not great, and emergency medical staff have difficulty getting him connected to the machines. I feel totally helpless at this moment. My husband and I spend Easter in hospital, sharing shifts and juggling work commitments.

The good news is that Caleb is now a healthy teenager and avid rock climber with aspirations to climb as many mountain ranges as he can. He has a trip planned to climb base camp of Mount Everest in Nepal which will undoubtedly test his fitness and lung capacity.

Asthma wasn't the only obstacle Caleb has faced in his life. He has experienced learning challenges because he has dyslexia. Learning about the brain has helped me work with Caleb's doctor and teachers, and my insight into neuroscience helped Caleb to understand that he has a greater capacity for creative thinking and problem solving because his brain operates differently to other people's.

My path to neuroscience

Mansur's death and Caleb's health challenges led me to a crisis point in my life. Everything was a struggle and my whole body felt heavy. Work was hectic with continued double-digit growth targets each year, and new product launches with less budget and resources. Building a successful career as a perfectionist was no longer sustainable, now I was also caring for a sick toddler. I felt like a failure at my job, as a wife, as a friend and as a mother. I was living on a diet of adrenaline, lack of sleep and tons of pressure to perform, with little fuel left in the tank. I was operating on autopilot and in a constant state of threat. I felt that I couldn't sustain my lifestyle without it having an impact on my social, mental and physical health.

Something had to give.

My 'AHA' moment of insight was reflecting on Mansur's death and realising that life is short, and we need to make the most of it. This is when I started to become curious and started searching for work / life balance career options.

The answer wasn't immediate. I worked for another two IT companies for a further six years, helping them to grow their revenue by 30 per cent. Finally, I realised that if I could contribute to these results for my employers, I could do this for myself, so I launched my own consulting business, Link Success, in 2013.

It was during the three-years I ran my own business that a client recommended I read some books on the neuroscience of leadership. Once I started reading, I could not put the books down.

My thinking was 'WOW.' I had been fascinated by how to achieve a sustainable work / life balance since losing Mansur and having a family. I was curious about how people could sustain crazy growth targets year on year without facing ill health and well-being. Understanding neuroscience gave me insight into how the brain operates and reacts in various situations. This changed my thinking, changed how I made decisions and allowed me to solve problems more effectively. I was hungry to learn as much as I could.

Studies I selected included an Advance Diploma in the Neuroscience of Leadership at NeuroCapability, NeuroTREAD™ accreditation with EnHansen Performance and PRISM Brain Mapping (behavioural profiling) accreditation. Completing these studies and programmes, changed my world and then it changed the world of my clients and friends in my community. It has enabled me to truly understand how different brains work.

Today I coach clients with all types of different learning requirements including visual impairment, attention deficit disorder (ADD) and attention deficit hyperactivity disorder (ADHD).

All of these life experiences and studies have led me to share my knowledge, passion and insights with you in this book. Everyone knows about conserving the environment, but I say I am in the business of human conservation promoting the balance between work, life and well-being. I want to help you discover what I have learned; life is an obstacle course, but one with many rich learnings, possibilities, and opportunities to grow.

How the Brain Works

How the brain works

We typically wander around with little understanding how our biggest asset works. Our brain operates on autopilot in the subconscious 95 per cent of the time.[1]

I believe we need to understand how our brain functions, performs and adapts to changing environments.

There are many unfounded myths about the brain, including:
Myth 1: We use only a small percentage of its capacity.
Myth 2: You can't teach old dogs new tricks.
Myth 3: Our brains are fixed by the time we reach adulthood.

The truth

We do have the capacity to leverage the whole brain by creating a new habit. To do this requires energy, focus, being in a reward state and repetition.

Our brains are not fixed in adulthood. You may have heard the phrase brain plasticity, also known as neuroplasticity. This term refers to the brain's ability to change and adapt as a result of experience.

For a long time, it was believed that as we age, the connections in the brain became fixed, and then simply faded. Research has now shown that the brain never stops changing through learning. Plasticity is the capacity of the brain to change with learning.

Neuroplasticity is the human brain's amazing ability to reorganise itself by forming new connections between brain cells (neurons). Learning new things is the key to our health and well-being, as it helps our brains form new connections.

In addition to genetic factors, the environment in which people live and their actions play a significant role in plasticity.

1. Daniel Kahneman, a Senior scholar at Princeton University, author of Thinking, fast and slow, 2011.

Let's look at some of the brain's core areas responsible for rational and emotional thinking, decision-making, innovative thinking and problem-solving.

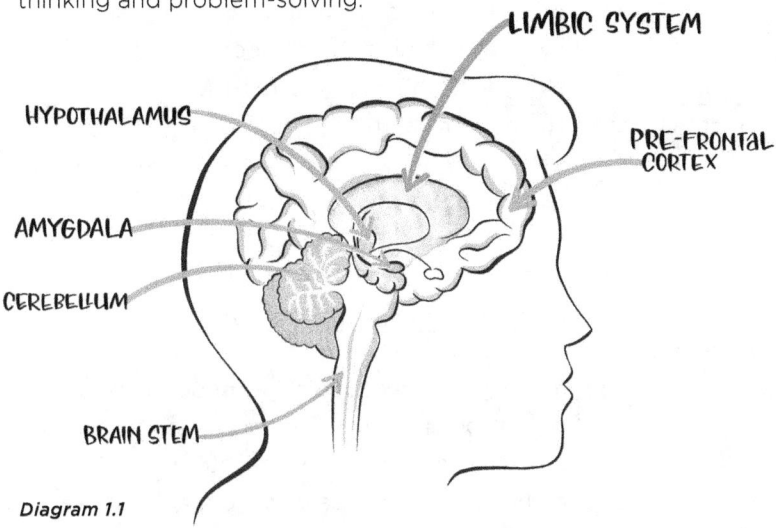

Diagram 1.1

Our brain is the most important asset we own. See diagram 1.1. I will explain some of the areas of the brain that come into play with functions such as leadership, decision-making, experiencing emotions and regulating emotions.

Brain Area	Description
Pre-frontal Cortex (PFC)	The PFC is the cerebral cortex covering the front part of the frontal lobe. This brain region is responsible for planning complex cognitive behaviour, personality expression, decision making, and moderating social behaviour. The basic activity of this brain region is considered to be orchestration of thoughts and actions in accordance with internal goals. The most typical psychological term for functions carried out by the prefrontal cortex area is executive function.

Limbic System	A component of the brain located above the brain stem that is responsible for three primary functions: emotion, memory, and arousal, including the hippocampus, the amygdala, and the hypothalamus.
Hypothalamus	The hypothalamus is in control of generating the body's numerous hormones. Consists of various stations which control the following functions: feeding, maintaining body temperature, control of water levels in the body and regulating sleep cycles.
Amygdala	An automatic response to physical danger that allows you to react quickly without thinking. When you feel threatened and afraid, the amygdala automatically activates the fight-flight-freeze response by sending out signals to release stress hormones that prepare your body to fight or run away. The name amygdala is derived from the Greek word, meaning 'almond', owing to the structure's almond like shape. The amygdala is part of the limbic system, a neural network that mediates many aspects of emotion and memory.
Cerebellum	Located at the back/bottom of the brain, behind the brainstem. Significant area used to function movement and coordination, including balance, motor learning, and vision.
Brain Stem	The heart rate, breathing, sleeping, and feeding are only a few of the essential processes of the brainstem. It also helps with conduction. The brainstem must carry all information from the body to the cerebrum and cerebellum, and vice versa.

Some basic facts about the brain

→ It weighs around 1.3–1.4kgs and consists of 73 per cent water
→ It consumes approximately 20 per cent of our oxygen and water intake
→ The two key ingredients for optimal Pre-frontal Cortex function, are glucose and oxygen
→ 95 per cent of the time our brain operates on auto-pilot and 5 per cent of the time we are conscious of thinking
→ Attention is a limited resource – the human body sends an estimated 11 million bits of information per second to the brain for processing, and the conscious mind can only process about 40 bits per second[2]. Imagine what would happen to us if we were consciously aware of 11 million bits of information per second? We would literally go into melt-down. Most of the body's activities take place outside direct conscious control, so practice and habit formation are important.

Prefrontal cortex (PFC)

The prefrontal cortex controls our executive function, it is the CEO of the brain. It is known as our thinking and conscious rational brain and is located behind our forehead. The PFC comprises approximately 4–6 per cent of the brain's size and is the part of the brain that has developed the most since primitive times.

What job functions use the prefrontal cortex (PFC)?

The PFC is involved with problem solving, judgement, working memory, planning, anticipation, expressive language, analysis, inhibition of behaviour aka behavioural control (inhibition – like stopping yourself from saying something you will later regret),

[2]. Norretanders 1998 and Wilson 2002.

organisation, attention, initiation and risk assessment – just to name a few. It is an essential part of the brain, despite its size.

The PFC has limitations. How many hours of key thinking time (productivity) do you think we have in a day? On average, the PFC can be used optimally for around three hours in a 24-hour period[3].

To optimise your PFC, it is vital to maximise your precious time and energy throughout your day. Your brain can be likened to a mobile phone; if you have lots of apps and windows open, it slows down, shuts down or needs rebooting and charging. Our brain is similar; it needs the right balance of fuel throughout the day and night to recharge. Back-to-back meetings, continuous emails and multi-tasking are some of the things that drain its energy resources.

The limbic system

The limbic system, located above the brain stem, is the brain's emotional centre, and every thought goes through this part of the brain. We are emotional beings that think and not the other way around. With a corporate career spanning over 20 years, I was taught that business is just business; there is nothing to get emotional about when decisions are made from the top of an organisation regardless of how they impact your targets for the year ahead. This is yet another gap between what science knows and what businesses do.

The amygdala sits above the brain stem and is a component part of the limbic centre responsible for our fight, flight, and freeze response.

Why do we have an amygdala? To keep us alive, for survival.

---

3. Korn Ferry survey 13 November, 2019. www.kornferry.com/about-us//press/working-or-wasting-time Los Angeles, Nov. 13, 2019 www.codebots.com/library/way-of-working/how-many-hours-a-day-are-workers-productive www.cnbc.com/2019/11/17/67percent-of-workers-say-spending-too-much-time-in-meetings-distracts-them.html

It is our threat and reward response, the brain's organising principle. If you imagined you were on a three-lane highway, travelling at 120 kilometres per hour, and your tyre blew, which part of the brain would save you fastest? Would it be your PFC, that analyses and thinks through your options or your amygdala designed to get you safe immediately? When you must make a decision quickly in life-threatening situations, it is likely your amygdala (our survival mechanism, subconscious and auto-pilot) that will get you out of this situation and to safety quickest.

The sympathetic nervous system is engaged when the brain detects a threat, triggering the so-called fight, flight, freeze reaction. Cortisol, a hormone that raises blood sugar and suppresses the immune system, is released, allowing energy to be transferred as a means of protecting against the perceived threat. Other hormones are released as well, including adrenaline (epinephrine), which raises heart rate, dilates bronchial airways, and constricts blood vessels, all in order to increase oxygen to the lungs and blood flow to muscles. You may feel your mouth go dry or your palms become sweaty when in a stressful situation, this means you're experiencing the sympathetic nervous system at work[4].

Think about a time you had a conflict with someone at work or at home. What was your thinking a couple of hours later? Did you think, "Why did I say what I did and why didn't I say this instead?" Depending on the severity of the threat, cortisol can block your rational thinking for a few hours or more. This means your emotional centre is in control, and your rational thought (executive / PFC action) is blocked and unable to inhibit your emotions.

---

4. ATD - Association for Talent Development article, The Neuroscience of Reward and Threat, 2016 www.td.org/insights/the-neuroscience-of-reward-and-threat

Flipping our lid (aka going limbic)

Have you ever heard of the concept of flipping your lid? It is something that happens within the brain when confronting a threat from the amygdala.

Dan Siegal, a clinical professor of psychiatry at the University of California, Los Angeles (UCLA) School of Medicine, author of several books and Director of the Mindsight Institute, has a simple explanation of the brain. It is so simple you can share it with children, but it also explains the relationship between our emotional and rational brain to adults effectively.

Professor Siegal explains that when we know what is going on in the brain, we can change what the brain does. The front part of the brain, the PFC, is the part that regulates the subcortical limbic and brain stem areas. This regulation is crucial because when we have things happen in our lives, such as being tired, exhausted, overwhelmed, and someone pushes an emotional button, we can flip our lids. Instead of being in tune, balanced and flexible, we can lose flexibility and reason and act in ways that are terrifying to others. Check out the reference section to view the clip[5], which is worth watching for the visual clues.

The amygdala

When we are busy, don't know what to do in a new role, or are learning a new technology, we can experience a situation that causes the amygdala to hijack control of our response to stress (aka the amygdala hijack). We let panic take over our thinking rather than proactively communicating in a positive manner. This response is triggered by emotions like fear, anxiety, aggression, and anger. Not only does it impact us, but also affects the people around us.

---

5. Dan Siegal, Clinical Professor of Psychiatry and author of several books and Director of the Mindsight Institute, has a really simple way of explaining the brain. Watch video www.youtube.com/watch?v=gm9ClJ74Oxw 2mins 31secs, 2012.

By actively stimulating your PFC, the reasoning, logical half of your brain, you can reduce or eliminate the symptoms of amygdala hijack. This may take considerable time and effort. If you make a mistake, it's okay; learn from it instead of bashing yourself up. Perfection does not exist, though learning is valuable and key for the brain's health long term.

It is a sign of the times that we are bombarded with loads of information, constant change, immediacy and heavy workloads. You can see a deadline as a threat (which chemically harnesses different activity in your brain), or you can see it as an opportunity to rise. You have a choice to either allow your brain to perceive things as a threat or see change as an opportunity.

Many neuroimaging experiments have shown that people with post-traumatic stress disorder (PTSD) have a greater level of amygdala activation[6].

The reward pathway

Two of the brain's key operating principles drive human actions: survival — food, sleep, avoidance of pain — and rewards. Any obstacle, event, or activity can be a reward if it motivates us, causes us to learn, or elicits pleasurable feelings. But how do our brains compute the value of a reward, and how is that translated into action? The answer lies in the brain circuitry known as the 'reward system.'

The reward pathway of the brain is connected to the areas that control behaviour and memory. It begins in the ventral tegmental area, where neurons release the neurotransmitter dopamine (the brain's natural happy / pleasure drug) to make you feel pleasure. The brain starts to make connections between the activity and the pleasure, ensuring that we will repeat the behaviour. Neurotransmitters are chemical

6. Biological Psychiatry article; Amygdala Activity, Fear, and Anxiety: Modulation by Stress, 2010.

substances made by the neuron specifically to transmit a message. See diagram 1.2[7].

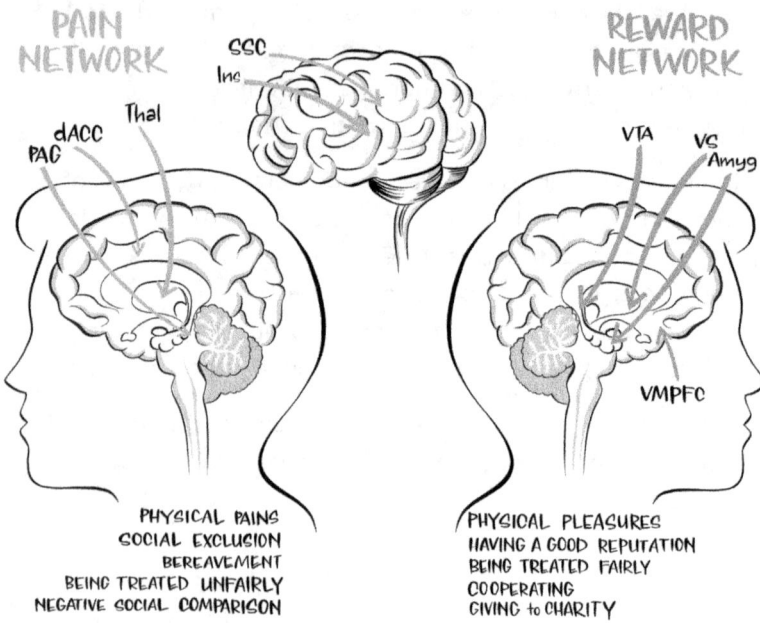

Diagram 1.2

The pain network consists of the dorsal anterior cingulate cortex (dACC), insula (Ins), somatosensory cortex (SSC), thalamus (Thal), and periaqueductal gray (PAG). This network is implicated in physical and social pain processes. The reward or pleasure network consists of the ventral tegmental area (VTA), ventral striatum (VS), ventromedial prefrontal cortex (VMPFC), and the amygdala (Amyg). This network is implicated in physical and social rewards.

Dopamine also enhances reward-related memories. It strengthens synapses — the junctions which neurons pass messages — in the brain's learning and memory centre or hippocampus. Dopamine signalling in areas of the brain that process emotions (the amygdala) and regions involved in planning and reasoning (the prefrontal cortex) also creates emotional associations between rewards.

7. Eisenberger & Lieberman, Pains and pleasures of social life, diagram sourced from sciencemag.org 2009.

It is not the reward itself, but the expectation of a reward that most powerfully influences emotional reactions and memories. Reward learning occurs when we experience something unexpected, when the actual reward differs from what we otherwise would predict. Suppose a reward is greater than anticipated, dopamine signalling increases. If a reward is less than expected, dopamine signalling decreases. In contrast, correctly predicting a reward does not alter dopamine signalling because we aren't learning anything new.

Dopamine responses vary from person to person. Some people's brains react more strongly to rewards than punishments, while others respond more strongly to punishments. The amygdala strongly influences reward learning and motivation.

Decision-making often involves evaluating risks in addition to rewards. Neuroscientists are investigating how the brain balances reward and risk and how your emotional state affects this balance.

Threat and reward responses have an impact on us, both physically and mentally. Compared with the reward response, the threat response tends to:

- speed the heart rate
- slow digestion
- release of hormones like adrenalin and cortisol
- shunt blood flow to major muscle groups
- impact other brain functions such as working memory, analytic thinking, creative insight and problem solving
- increase emotional response[8].

 **Just do it:**

List the emotional triggers for flipping your lid. If you know what the most common ones are, you can be more aware as you feel

---

8. Young Diggers article; The fight or flight response: Our body's response to stress, 2010 www.youngdiggers.com.au/fight-or-flight; Strategy+Business article; Managing with the Brain and Mind, 2009 www.strategy-business.com/article/09306

your emotions rise, which allows you to get in early enough to take a break. Name how you feel, increase your oxygen intake and re-evaluate by asking yourself, "How else can I see this situation or what are the potential learnings for growth or how can I view this from the other person's perspective?"

Common client & team threat trigger examples:

- → Having an overloaded inbox
- → Being late for important meetings
- → Being unprepared or having limited notice to be prepared
- → Facing challenging situations such as dealing with a conflict between differing opinions, values and beliefs
- → Having short notice deadlines and blaming others for missing deadlines
- → Undergoing performance reviews
- → Being hungry or dehydrated, when in back-to-back continuous meetings
- → Multi-tasking, or having to do multiple things quickly and not as well as you can because of limited time provided
- → Having an excessive workload
- → Doing multiple people's roles due to resource shortages
- → Unplugging from remote working (feeling like Ground Hog Day).

My threat triggers are when people blame others, not feeling I am adding value, wasting time, feeling I'm being taken for granted, and not having my needs for emotional connection met.

Perhaps these examples may get you curious about what your threat triggers are?

Being more aware of and probing why these triggers are important to you is helpful because they are usually instantaneous and controlled by your subconscious (reminder - we are on autopilot 95 per cent of the time).

Common reward trigger examples include:

- Being prepared and organised
- Establishing positive connections with colleagues which mean you can have a laugh together
- Being acknowledged for a job well done
- Receiving recognition through an excellence award
- Seeing people doing amazing work and collaborating effectively with other teams
- Receiving positive client feedback
- Achieving a goal
- Witnessing those in your team reaching their goals
- Getting to do what you are most passionate about
- Making a difference in the lives of others
- Being asked for your opinion and expertise.

My reward triggers include being recognised by my clients, family and friends for making a difference in their lives. Winning new client deals and accomplishing my goals provide me with big hits of dopamine.

What are your reward triggers? How could you increase them throughout your week?

Not all stress is harmful

Whilst it is clear that there can be serious outcomes from prolonged exposure to stress, some relatively new research suggests that stress can be good for you. It would seem our mindset about stress – whether we view it as harmful or as helpful – can profoundly influence how our body and brain react to stressors. Kelly McGonigal, a health psychologist, lecturer at Stanford University and author of *The Upside of Stress*[9], suggests we view stress differently.

McGonigal shows how to make stress your friend and provides research that supports the theory that if we change our mindset about stress, we can change the impact it has on us. The research she refers to in her TED talk (listed in the references section) studied 30,000 adults over eight years. The study asked two questions – how much stress have you experienced in the past year, and do you believe stress is harmful? Subsequently, the researchers examined death records to see who amongst the participants had died. People who reported that they experienced a lot of stress in the previous year and thought stress was harmful, had a 43 per cent increased risk of dying. Those people who experienced a lot of stress, but didn't see it as harmful, were no more likely to die. Other researchers refer to the importance of stress mindset and suggest we can have either a 'stress is debilitating mindset', or a 'stress is enhancing mindset'.

---

9. Kelly McGonigal is a health psychologist and lecturer at Stanford University who is known for her work in the field of 'science help' which focuses on translating insights from psychology and neuroscience into practical strategies that support health and well-being. Author of the upside of stress, www.youtube.com/watch?v=IaVKXx767rw 3:34 sec video, 2015.

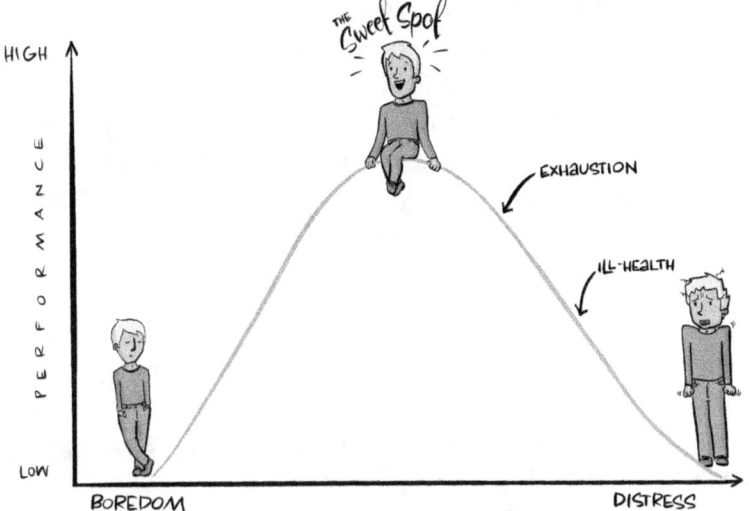

Diagram 1.3

Stress hormones and performance

In 1908, Robert Yerkes and John Dodson examined the range between our arousal and performance. The Yerkes-Dodson law suggests that our performance on any task will be poor when our arousal is low (an indicator of boredom) and too much stress may lead to distress / chronic stress[10] that has a shrinking effect on the PFC, the area of the brain responsible for memory and learning. As we get more aroused, i.e. motivated, excited and engaged, our performance picks up to a peak point, the brain's sweet spot.

The sweet spot for performance is at the top of the inverted U in diagram 1.3. This is where people work at their best, think at their best. This is where people experience flow, referred to as being in a state of neural harmony. It's also a state of maximum cognitive efficiency when we are performing at our very best.

10. Turo university Worldwide article 'The Mind and Mental Health: How stress affects the brain.'
www.tuw.edu/health/how-stress-affects-the-brain

At work, or when you're doing something you care about, that's where you want to be and where you want people you are working with to be because that is where you get the best out of people. You want people to be in the middle in the sweet spot. It is vital to remember that no two brains are alike, which means that different stimuli will arouse people. No two people have the same arousal response, so identifying people's triggers provides valuable insights.

As mentioned, it is impossible to be in the sweet spot for huge amounts of time as our energy and attentional focus runs out of gas. That's why planning the structure of your day is imperative. Consider the time of day you do your best thinking, and when you work, take brain breaks at least every 45-60 mins for 5-15 minutes and increase your oxygen during these breaks. Communicate with others when you are doing your deep thinking, so they don't unnecessarily interrupt, and turn off devices, messaging sounds and pop-up messages. It is also crucial to allocate time for the unknown throughout your day. In my experience, there is always something that changes or happens or people that need your attention. See section 2 'Organise your daily structure based on when you do your best thinking' for more information and tips.

Just do it:

Answer the following questions:
- What does your performance sweet spot look and feel like?
- How long can you keep your attentional focus for?
- When does it make sense to add 5-15 minute brain breaks throughout your day to re-energise?
- What activities could you do in your 5-15 minute brain breaks that allow you to increase your oxygen uptake?
- What strategies could minimise internal and external distractions during your sweet spot?

- What does high stress look-like for you?
- What are common distress triggers for you?
- How could you minimise high stress and perceive it differently?

It is okay if you don't have answers to all these questions yet. I recommend coming back to this page as you continue reading.

Working from home during COVID presented a mix of benefits and challenges (stressors). The main benefits were increases in productivity, flexibility, autonomy, focus, work-life balance and reduced commute time by at least six hours per week. Some of my clients saved 20 hours a week with reduced commute time, which was fantastic.

Some of the challenges were setting up technology remotely, internet bandwidth, loneliness, miscommunication or a lack of communication, too much information, back-to-back meetings, no brainstorming ideas over the water cooler, in the office kitchen or sharing a coffee, and distractions with other household members working and schooling from home.

Several of my clients found that unplugging after work, managing exhausting back-to-back video conferencing calls and inadequate exercise throughout the day was detrimental to their overall health and fitness. One client gained 15 kilograms in three months and is now doing the hard yards training and dieting, which is initially harsh on the body.

If you have some of these challenges, I will provide some more ideas for your consideration throughout the book.

Strategic decision making

Interestingly, intuition, also known as a gut feel, (which I have always found fascinating) is located in the limbic system. There is no language in this part of the brain, so people sometimes refer to intuition as gut feel. I have often heard executives comment, "I know the data is telling me to decide in a particular direction, but my gut feel tells me it's not the right choice." Some of the best strategic thinkers show more activity in parts of the brain linked with emotion and intuition.

Interesting research from Asana Anatomy of Work Index 2021[11] shows that only 13 per cent of Australian and New Zealand workers' time is spent on forward-looking strategy. Asana is a web and mobile application designed to help teams organise, track, and manage their work. I have been a spokesperson for Asana providing brain friendly solutions to the Anatomy of Work Index 2021 results.

How important is strategic decision making for you in your current work? Would you like to improve in this area? Are you curious about what this could look like for you in the future?

What's involved with change

Change is all around us and often happens in a short period of time. It's an inevitable part of life. Some people thrive on change, but for others, it's very stressful. How often do we really think about how our brains deal with change? Why change is sometimes challenging to deal with? How we can more effectively manage change?

We operate in a world that doesn't stand still and is becoming increasingly complex, so it is crucial to understand our environment. We need to value and encourage innovation and see change as an opportunity, not something that needs to be managed in prescriptive ways. However, we haven't yet adapted sufficiently to deal with increased complexity.

---

11. Asana Anatomy of Work Index 2021. Accessed from: www.asana.com/resources/anatomy-of-work In October 2020, quantitative research was conducted by Sapio Research on behalf of Asana, to understand how people spend time at work.

Many people are frightened by the thought of change. Perhaps we need to alter our language by replacing the word 'change' with names such as organisational growth, vitality, and innovation. Organisational 'CHANGE Projects' shouldn't have finite time frames but should be continuously evolving.

Our brain works hard to decide if a reward is significant enough to warrant the energy hungry process of changing. The brain is an energy conserving organ and will resist change because it takes cognitive effort and uses up valuable oxygen and glucose resources. Fundamental to change are the judgements we make about whether to act or not to act, based on the sum of risk value + reward value. The result should be positive in the affirmative.

This means if we perceive the reward to be unworthy of the risk, we are unlikely to engage in change. The brain will decide it's not worth the effort. Therefore, it is critical to share the WHY of change to help people see the benefits of spending large amounts of precious cognitive resources in a change process. As the brain is wired to detecting threat / risk, the reward needs to be perceived as significant.

Because the brain loves to predict what will happen next, providing certainty is very important to the success of a change process. It is often overlooked and undervalued in the change process. With change, managers seem to assume that everything will be okay, and they don't deal with the uncertainty that change can create for most people.

We need people to feel certain about the purpose, benefits and steps involved in the change, and mitigate any potential risks, so their brains perceive the change as worth the effort (the reward for changing!). People need to feel that it is okay to do something new and different that they haven't experienced before, without feeling frightened.

Just do it:

What have you observed about how you deal with change? How could you see change in a different way?

The basis of neuroplasticity

One of neuroscience's most significant discoveries is neuroplasticity. This is the brain's ability to adapt just like malleable soft plastic can change shape. How does it work? Think of your brain as a dynamic power grid, with billions of neural pathways or roads lighting up every time you think, feel or do something. Some of these roads are well travelled; these are our habits. These are our established ways of thinking, feeling and doing.

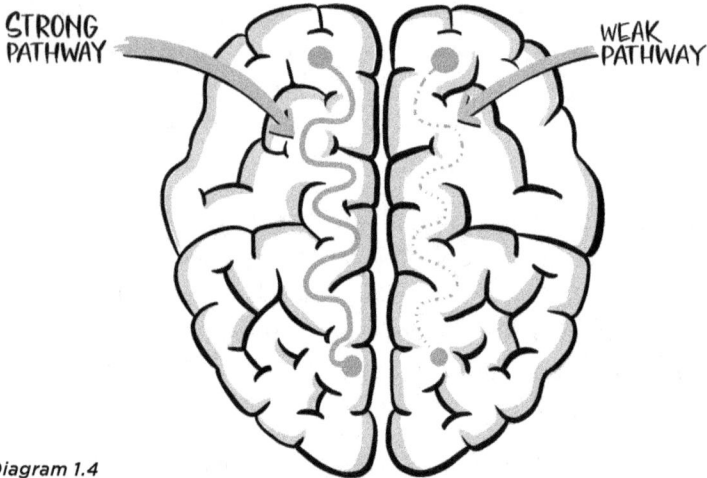

Diagram 1.4

Every time we think in a certain way, practise a particular way of doing something or feel a specific emotion, we strengthen these neural roads, and it becomes easier for our brains to travel them. This saves neural energy – as our brain is an energy demanding organ. When we learn a new task or emotion, we carve out a new road. As we focus more on a new habit, the old road weakens (see diagram 1.4). This process of rewiring our brain by forming new connections (new roads) and weakening old ones is neuroplasticity in action.

"Neuroplasticity can be defined as brain's ability to change, remodel and reorganise for purpose of better ability to adapt to new situations". Vida Demarin, Neuropsychiatry[12].

 Just do it:

We often have behavioural habits that no longer serve us in this busy digital age. What is one behavioural change you would like to make? What would it look like to achieve it? Write it down, and we will review this later in other sections.

---

12. V Demarin, S Morovic, R Béné. Neuroplasticity. Periodicum Biologorum. 2014;116(2):209-211.

SECTION ONE

The F.O.O.D Framework

Section One – The F.O.O.D framework

My F.O.O.D framework consists of proven models of behaviour, health, wellbeing and adaptability to help you achieve a work / life balance.

It is estimated that the absenteeism in Australian workplaces is approximately 9.7 days of unplanned leave per year, which costs the economy $44 billion annually[13]. In America, over one million people call in sick every day due to work-related stress, according to the American Institute of Stress[14]. Numerous studies show that job stress is far and away the major source of stress for adults and that is has escalated progressively over the past few decades.

The F.O.O.D framework stands for:

Fuel your brain with the right ingredients

Organise your daily structure based on when you do your best thinking

Overcome obstacles with the brain in mind

Drive the right behaviours, mindset and passion for achieving your desired outcomes.

The F.O.O.D framework explains the ingredients that contribute to a healthy full-functioning brain and body, with different options as no two brains are the same. What works is different from one person to the next, so select the options that align best for your brain and body.

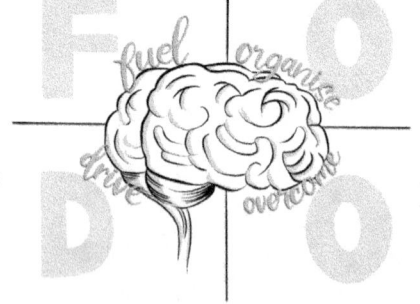

---

13. Sources: DHS 2017 Absence Management and Wellbeing Survey Report; AiG Absenteeism & Presenteeism Survey Report 2015; AHRI HR Pulse Survey - Absence Management, 2016; Robert Half 2016 Survey; WorkplaceInfo.
14. www.stress.org/workplace-stress

I have collaborated with experts in my network throughout this section, to bring you rich flavours of information; taste and digest what you need. If you want to explore any of these topics in more depth, each expert's details appear below their contribution and within the references and resources section at the back of the book.

Fuel your brain with the right ingredients

Our brain is a supercomputer that relies on rich energy resources I refer to as fuel. It is the biggest asset we own, and it needs a lot of energy to operate effectively as we navigate our busy lives.

How we top up our energy throughout our day is especially important when dealing with obstacles and change. Why? Because we need more energy resources to adapt and avoid becoming distressed which can cause shifts in the balance of neurochemicals that either support our capacity to adapt or the opposite, such as being dogmatic and stubborn.

In my experience, the way many of us currently fuel our brain and how we use it throughout the day generally depletes our energy resources. This is why we can feel tired and exhausted at certain times of the day and the end of the week. By the time we get to Friday night, many people don't have much energy or cognitive function left, and if you have busy weekends, too, you may not have had time to re-energise. So, you start the next week without a fully restored battery, which, over time, can lead to exhaustion and ill-health.

There are many ways to refuel, and I will explain options that have successfully worked for me, my family and my clients.

In summary, we cover the following ingredients:

→ **Diet**
What you eat and drink is fundamental to how your body and brain functions, including how you feel within yourself. Food is the fuel that gives your body and brain energy – if you don't choose the right ingredients, you won't have the energy to fully function on all levels.

→ **Exercise**
Physical activity has been fundamental to the survival of the human race and is a cornerstone of a healthy life. Increasing our oxygen levels helps us rejuvenate our body and brain, allowing us to build resilience and bounce back from obstacles.

→ **Sleep**
We sleep for approximately one-third of our lives. The quality of our sleep influences the quality of the time we are awake.

- **Social connection**
  Humans are born to connect, regardless of whether we have introverted or extroverted personalities. It is more than just physical needs; we are emotionally, cognitively, and spiritually hardwired for connection, love, and belonging.

- **Mindfulness**
  Paying attention to the present moment without judgement, allows us to rest our mind and body. It improves our wellbeing and relieves stress.

- **Music therapy**
  Music can boost cognition function and connect both hemispheres of the brain, facilitating more effective retrieval of information from each side of the brain. Music also can be a great strategy for relieving stress, improving mental health and reducing a threat response.

- **Rest, Recovery and Relaxation**
  Nurturing our body and brain is perhaps one of the most worthwhile investments that we can make. Rest, recovery and relaxation are essential.

Maximising your energy consumption by considering your DIET

Healthy eating is essential for memory, mood and focus because the brain uses more than 20 per cent of our caloric needs. It has long been suspected that specific nutrients can affect cognitive processes and emotions.

Although food has classically been perceived as a means of providing energy to the body and brain, its ability to prevent and protect against diseases is increasingly being recognised. In particular, research over the past five years has provided compelling evidence of the influence of dietary factors on specific molecular systems and mechanisms that maintain cognitive function.

Over thousands of years, diet and other aspects of daily living, such as exercise, has played a crucial role in shaping cognitive capacity and brain evolution.

My family is interested in diet as we are all drawn to physical performance. My son's passion is rock climbing; my husband is interested in cross-fit and for me, it's dancing. None of us are good cooks, so we're always looking for easy and healthy options.

Through working with my clients, I understand the link between fueling the brain with the right nutrition and workplace performance. I ask them what time of day their energy is at its lowest.

Now I ask you to do the same!

If you need to do cognitive thinking in the afternoon, having a carbohydrate-heavy lunch is likely to make you feel sleepy and sluggish. No matter how important your afternoon meetings and projects are, you're unlikely to perform at your best.

If eating nuts is safe for you, a handful of almonds or protein for a morning snack can come in handy for perking up your cognitive function. I carry small bags of almonds with me in my handbag in case I feel like I need an energy boost between meetings or before doing cognitive tasks or keynote presentations.

Another way to support your brain's cognitive function is to stay hydrated throughout your day. Regularly sipping fluid is best as sculling results in the fluid going straight to your bladder. Water can get boring, so I suggest people experiment by adding a few drops of fresh lemon or lime, chlorophyll, slices of cucumber, chopped mint or herbal teas. For me, chamomile tea and a few drops of chlorophyll in my glass of water get me going in the morning, and peppermint tea and a few drops of lemon or lime in my water gets me through the afternoon.

I have invited two nutrition experts to join me to collaborate and contribute to this section of **Rewire for Success**. Introducing you to nutritionist and naturopath, Kerrin Booth, and nutritional neuroscientist and stress resiliency consultant, Dr Delia McCabe.

I first met Kerrin when my infant son, Caleb, had just been diagnosed with severe asthma. Kerrin recommended a natural diet to help build Caleb's strength and health. When Caleb was diagnosed with dyslexia in Year 4, Kerrin created a diet plan that would support his cognitive function. Kerrin's advice helped our son develop into a healthy and fit young man who is very conscious about what he eats. He knows that nutrition is a critical component of his challenging rock-climbing goals. When my husband and I went to school, our lunch mainly consisted of vegemite sandwiches, but these days Caleb has gourmet salads with protein for school lunches.

Kerrin Booth - Nutritionist, Naturopath

Wired but tired?
How to keep your brain alert but calm

What you eat and drink is fundamental to how your body and brain functions. Food is the fuel that gives your body and brain energy – if you don't choose the right ingredients, you won't have the energy to fully function on all levels. Food also contains the vitamins and minerals essential for energy production and is vital to energy regulation and our stress response. We need to eat good, nutritious food regularly.

Three nutritious meals every day is a great start. If your life is so erratic that you are not doing this, bringing balance into your eating pattern is a good start to bringing balance into your life. Protein is key to maintaining good blood sugar balance, and it stabilises your mood, keeps you feeling satisfied and provides your body with nutrients.

Include protein in your breakfast. Eggs are a great start to the day, as are yoghurt with some nuts and seeds, muesli containing nuts and seeds, good quality wholemeal rye toast with hummus and avocado, sardines or baked beans on toast. If you eat a refined high sugar breakfast cereal for breakfast, you will have very short-lived energy and sugar cravings all day, combined with highs and lows of blood sugar levels. This will lead to highs and lows in moods.

To avoid an afternoon slump, cut down on the carbohydrates for lunch and stick with protein (meat, chicken, fish, egg, beans or legumes) and a salad or vegetables. Mid-afternoon, have a protein-based snack such as a handful of nuts, or a piece of chicken or tin of tuna if you are hungry. This should help keep your energy levels and moods on track for the afternoon.

Eat dinner as early as you can rather than straight before bed. There is a lot of research validating the benefits of fasting overnight – making as much time between dinner and breakfast as possible (at least 12 hours or more) – and how beneficial this is in preventing chronic health problems including cardiovascular disease. Eating dinner early also gives your body a more restful and restorative sleep, as it is not spending all that time and energy on digesting. Good sleep is so important and cutting back on alcohol will also help with a more refreshing sleep. Many people think alcohol helps them sleep better, but it changes sleep patterns and reduces the deeper, more restorative part of the sleep cycle.

Remember to drink water. If you're feeling thirsty, your body is already dehydrated. You need to drink water to prevent that feeling of thirst and dehydration. The general recommendation is to drink two litres of water per day. Your brain is approximately 75 per cent water and even mild dehydration affects mood and cognitive function, including concentration and alertness. Dehydration can cause lapses in attention and memory. Try to drink water away from meals, as drinking with meals can dilute and flush out digestive juices, leading to poor absorption of nutrients. The recommendation is not to drink for half an hour before food or one-hour after meals.

Caffeinated drinks do not count as water, although herbal teas do. Caffeine intake should not exceed two cups of coffee or tea per day. There are many adverse effects of drinking too much caffeine, including contributing to the 'tired but wired' feeling. Caffeine has been shown to make people feel more stressed, and it gives a 'false' energy by overstimulating the nervous system. In the long term, this leads to further exhaustion and more reliance on that stimulating effect. Make sure not to have caffeine too late in the day, as it can interfere with sleep if consumed after 2.00pm.

The end product of constant stress is what we call adrenal exhaustion. Your adrenal glands are responsible for providing stress hormones, and when they are constantly called upon, they become overworked. This results in a reduced ability to cope with stress. Certainly, reducing stress levels helps with this, and there are also some wonderful herbal medicines called adaptogens, which help the body adapt to and cope with stress (the ginsengs fall into this category of herbs). The adrenal glands also require large amounts of vitamin C, and this vitamin is essential for immune function.

B vitamins are essential to add to the repertoire for those who are wired and tired, as they are involved in producing energy, regulating blood sugar levels and supporting the nervous system. A deficiency of B group vitamins can contribute to depression and anxiety. Magnesium is another key nutrient to support and relax the nervous system and take the edge off stress.

Kerrin Booth graduated as a Naturopath in 1992, and her practice uses nutrition, herbal medicine and Australian Bush Flower Essences to help a wide variety of health problems.
www.kerrinboothnaturopath.com

....

Dr Delia McCabe, neuroscientist and stress resiliency consultant, has dedicated years to studying the latest in nutritional neuroscience and has written Feed your Brain and Feed your Brain Cookbook. Delia and I met through a common friend, who is also passionate about mental and physical health, and introduced Delia as one of the smartest brains around and she is. It is a delight collaborating with her and supporting each other's work.

Dr Delia McCabe - Stress Resiliency Consultant

Nutritional neuroscience

We need to seriously consider that the brain is responsive to our lifestyle choices. If we don't, the brain will become less efficient at performing the tasks we take for granted over time, because it becomes less capable of keeping itself structurally sound.

Thinking occurs across a sensitive, sophisticated, and vast network of specialised cells, called neurons. Each of these 83+ billion neurons rely on specific lifestyle choices, including what food we eat, to function effectively. One of the simplest and quickest ways to improve brain health is to focus on eating foods that support both the optimal structure and function of neurons. Robust evidence supports the idea that what we eat impacts our brain in a long-reaching and profound way.

Macronutrients comprise carbohydrates, fats, and proteins, all of which play critical roles in brain structure and function.

The preferred source of fuel for brain energy is glucose, sourced from the carbohydrates we consume. The brain uses over 20 per cent of the glucose we source from carbohydrates, more so if we experience chronic stress. All carbohydrates are not created equal, though, with processed carbohydrates containing more energy, but fewer micronutrients and fibre than unprocessed carbohydrates. They also contain additives and fats that have been damaged via food processing, all of which undermine brain function.

Consuming the right fats is critically important for brain health, with 60 per cent of the dry weight of the brain comprising fat. Of that 60 per cent, 20-25 per cent should be made up of essential fatty acids (EFAs). EFAs have a unique biochemical structure, which ensures the electrochemical impulses that drive communication between neurons are optimised. EFAs also play a significant role in the synthesis and release of neurotransmitters and the structure and functioning of neuronal membranes.

Unfortunately, our diet has become devoid of these essential compounds, and research suggests this lack negatively impacts the development of the young brain. It also impacts mature and aging brain function. EFAs are also very delicate fats, which means that many of these forms of fat that people consume today are damaged.

Protein comprises small compounds called amino acids, which are combined in specific ways with micronutrients, to create messengers, or neurotransmitters, which allow neurons to communicate with each other. Protein is also responsible for the synthesis of hormones and neuronal membrane structure. Although debates about various dietary choices, such as that between vegetarians and meat-eaters, are unlikely to be silenced in the foreseeable future, all protein sources from plants and animals are broken down into proteins' constituent parts, amino acids. A well-balanced vegetarian diet can therefore support optimal brain function. However, some vegetarian or vegan diets can be deficient in some micronutrients that are critically important for brain development and function.

Micronutrients comprise vitamins and minerals, such as B vitamins, antioxidants, and minerals, including, among others, iron, magnesium and zinc. Micronutrients perform a multitude of functions within the body and brain including acting as co-factors in conversion of macronutrients into fuel, hormones and neurotransmitters. Genetic anomalies can impact the availability of specific micronutrients sourced from food, negatively affecting brain function. Research suggests that symptoms of a deficiency in specific micronutrients first manifest in psychological symptoms, and later in physical ailments.

Toxic foods

Manufactured foods, produced with shelf life and profit in mind, do not support optimal brain health. Not only are such processed foods lacking in macro and micronutrients, but they also include additives that research suggests cause neurological damage. Although the blood-brain barrier may initially prevent them from entering the brain directly, damage to the gut lining leads to inflammation and brain damage can occur as a secondary consequence. In addition, processed foods contain damaged fats which impact brain function, due to the critical role that fats play in brain health.

Unfortunately, the palatability of processed foods makes them highly addictive, as do the compounds released upon absorption. This also supports a psychological attraction, which results in a robust neural pathway that drives ongoing consumption.

Toxic compounds, such as pesticides, also contribute to brain damage, due to their affinity to, and accumulation in, fat-rich tissue, such as brain tissue.

Gut health

Gut and brain health are intimately related, with a growing body of evidence suggesting that what crosses the gut lining either supports or undermines brain health. Once again, processed food plays a negative role in gut health because it disturbs the ratio between various types of bacteria present in the gut. Stress and poor sleep also tip the ratio in favour of those gut bacteria that should not proliferate beyond specific levels. As a result, specific bacteria become compromised and can no longer optimally support and protect the integrity of the gut lining. The digestion and absorption of food becomes compromised and no longer occurs with ease. A damaged gut lining triggers an inflammatory cascade that causes the release of compounds that cross the lining, into the blood stream and subsequently invade the brain. Furthermore, up to 80 per cent of our serotonin[15] should be produced in the gut, namely peripheral serotonin. Therefore, when gut integrity is comprised, so is serotonin synthesis, which leads to a cascade of negative neurobiological effects.

Nutritional cost of stress is high and far reaching

Our brain evolved to respond quickly and efficiently to any threat to our physical survival via adrenaline synthesis. We can run away from danger, stay and fight for survival, or stand very still (the freeze response), in the hope of being overlooked. However, our brains cannot tell the difference between a real, physical threat, or a perceived, psychological one, although the adrenalin produced was meant to spur physical activity. Psychological stress doesn't drive physical activity and excess adrenaline and cortisol production leads to neuronal death and prevents the growth of new neurons.

Regardless of where or what the stressor is, a number of B vitamins, antioxidants and minerals are involved in adrenaline and cortisol synthesis. When stress becomes chronic, nutrients

---

15. Serotonin is also known as 5-hydroxytryptamine (5-HT), acts both as neurotransmitter and hormone and is mainly found in the brain, bowels and blood platelets. Serotonin stabilises our mood, feelings of well-being, and happiness. It enables brain cells and other nervous system cells to communicate with each other. Serotonin also helps with sleeping, eating, and digestion – 31 Dec 2018.

are naturally diverted to stress hormone synthesis, as survival is more important than, for example, sleep, which serotonin ushers in. Over time, physical and mental exhaustion develops, along with other more serious ailments, as neither the body nor the brain can thrive with stress hormone synthesis overriding other, life-enhancing and healing activities.

Coffee is often used to increase energy levels when it's in short supply due to chronic stress. However, it increases energy via the release of adrenalin, so is a poor substitute for increasing energy levels sustainably. Despite the positive cognitive effects that research suggests accompanies coffee consumption, its effects on chronically stressed people have not been examined thoroughly.

In conclusion, one of the quickest ways to improve brain function is to ensure our diet becomes a brain supporting one. When such strategies are implemented, gut health naturally improves too, which also supports brain function. Finally, deprivation should not accompany the decision to eat for brain health. In fact, feeling deprived will derail the best attempts to change food choices and entrench new habits. The goal is to consume brain-supporting foods that also taste delicious.

Delia received her PhD from Adelaide Medical School and has immersed herself in the fascinating world of nutritional neuroscience. She offers a focused, insightful, evidence-based approach into how specific foods can improve our mood, concentration, memory and learning ability and help us manage stress and remain calm and happy in our busy, stressful world, regardless of our age.
www.lighterbrighteryou.life

Your brain loves exercise

Exercise has always been an essential part of my life and that of my family. Over the last few years, my husband and I have had a few injuries and health issues that have taken us away from our regular exercise routine. We have noticed our mental resilience – how we respond to obstacles – has been affected.
I realise we are conditioned and addicted to exercise.

Recently I had early-stage skin cancer removed from the back of my right calf, which restricted my regular exercise for almost six weeks. In the first week of my recovery, I was already climbing the walls and driving my husband and son crazy. I would flip my lid over simple things. Since being back at the gym and dancing again, I feel alive, and I'm so grateful to be able to move my body how I wish, with no limitations or restrictions.

I am now introducing you to Dr Craig Duncan, one of the world's leading human performance scientists with extensive experience in high-performance sport.

....

Dr Craig Duncan - Human Performance Scientist

Exercise and the Brain

Exercise or physical activity has been fundamental to the survival of the human race and is a cornerstone of a healthy life. Without physical activity, our ancestors would never have been able to escape life-threatening situations or find food. However, in our modern world, less than 25 per cent of people get the recommended 150 minutes of moderate exercise a week.

Are you one of the 25 or 75 per cent?

The benefits of exercise include the prevention and management of numerous health issues including stroke, type 2 diabetes, high blood pressure, depression, anxiety, many types of cancer, falls and arthritis. Furthermore, exercise also positively affects mood, weight control, sleep and energy levels.

The advantages of regular exercise are substantial. Although when we think about being physically active, it is mostly the physical changes we strive for, it is the benefits to our brain that may have the most positive overall impact. Regular physical activity improves cognitive processes, memory and overall brain health. Throughout our lifespan, daily physical activity is imperative for the development of our brain. Even preschool children (two to five years) need physical activity, not only to enhance growth and development but because 'play' enhances mental capacity and socialisation. Physical activity can also positively impact diseases most associated with our senior population, including Alzheimer's and Parkinson's.

Stress is an enormous cost to our society, and even I became a victim of a stress-related condition. In 2013, while working as a manager of human performance for a professional sporting team, I failed to listen to my own advice and had a near-fatal heart attack. Although I had been exercising regularly, I wasn't listening to my own body and pushed myself over my limit. It was an interesting outcome as stress had led me to make a poor exercise decision which led to my heart issues. Even so, if I had been less healthy, the chances of a fatal outcome would have been much higher.

There are many modes of exercise, and it's vital to choose the most appropriate activity for your needs. In my situation, because my stress levels were high, I needed a more relaxing activity. Instead, I took my frustration out on the weights I was lifting, and just tried to lift more than my capacity.

So, it is vital that not only do we exercise but that we do the right exercise.

Chronic physical activity increases your serotonin levels, which may positively impact depression and susceptibility to depression in later life. Aerobic-type exercise such as walking, cycling, swimming, running, and tennis increases blood flow to the brain, which enhances cognitive function and slows the impact of aging further.

Recent research has also confirmed that exercise can increase neural growth factors, including brain-derived neurotrophic factor (BDNF) which stimulates neurogenesis. These changes can reduce brain deterioration and positively impact learning and overall cognitive importance. Exercise is a simple and cost-effective method to maintain brain function and promote brain plasticity.

Exercise or any physical activity is essential for us to flourish and will positively impact all systems of the human body. As the brain is key to our overall performance and survival, we must maintain this most precious organ's integrity, particularly as we age. Regular exercise is not only the answer for positive physical aging but also for our cognitive processes.

Let's focus on increasing the percentage of people who exercise regularly, starting with you and those closest to you.

Dr Craig Duncan, a sports performance scientist, led the performance science teams that directly contributed to the drought-breaking winning performance of the NSW State of Origin team (2014 and 2018). Dr Duncan was awarded Australian Sports Scientist of the year (ESSA-2014).
www.drcraigduncan.com.au

Dancing and the brain

As Dr Craig Duncan mentioned, there are many modes of exercise, and it's vital to choose the most appropriate activity for your needs and that you enjoy.

I am known as the Zumba Queen amongst my friends and family. Dancing has been a passion of mine since I was a kid; something that has connected me to a diverse range of people and cultures over the years, including corporate team kick-offs in countries worldwide. Zumba for me is fun, it is like going to a dance party, the exercise and increase in cognitive function is a bonus.

Dancing has been an important part of my health and well-being, along with yoga, breathing techniques, strength and conditioning, healthy balanced diet and mindfulness practices.

Stimulating movement

Scientists gave little thought to the neurological effects of dance until relatively recently, when researchers began investigating the complex mental coordination that dance requires. In a 2008 article in Scientific American magazine[16], a Columbia University neuroscientist posited that synchronizing music and movement — dance, essentially — constitutes a 'pleasure double play'. Music stimulates the brain's reward centres, while dance activates its sensory and motor circuits.

Studies using PET imaging (Positron Emission Tomography) have identified regions of the brain that contribute to dance learning and performance. These regions include the motor cortex, somatosensory cortex, basal ganglia, and cerebellum. The motor cortex is involved in the planning, control, and

16. MIND & BRAIN article on Why do we like to dance - And move to the beat? www.scientificamerican.com/article/experts-dance September, 2008.

execution of voluntary movement. The somatosensory cortex, located in the brain's mid region, is responsible for motor control and plays a role in eye-hand coordination. The basal ganglia (known as the habit centre), a group of structures deep in the brain, work with other brain regions to smoothly coordinate movement. Simultaneously, the cerebellum integrates input from the brain and spinal cord and helps in the planning of fine and complex motor actions.

Movement as a therapy

Dance has been found to be therapeutic for patients with Parkinson's disease, a progressive neurological movement disorder, which develops when dopamine-producing cells in the brain are declining. The chemical, dopamine, is an essential component of the brain's system for controlling movement and coordination. As Parkinson's disease progresses, an increasing number of these cells die off, drastically reducing the amount of dopamine available to the brain.

According to a 2015 Harvard Medical School article 'Dancing and the brain'[17], dance has such beneficial effects on the brain that it is now being used to treat people with Parkinson's disease. "There's no question, anecdotally at least, that music has a very stimulating effect on physical activity," says Daniel Tarsy, MD, an HMS professor of neurology and director of the Parkinson's Disease and Movement Disorders Center at Beth Israel Deaconess Medical Center (BIDMC). "And this can apply to dance, as well."

Dance boosts memory

Dancing improves brain function and boosts memory. Several studies have shown that dancing is linked to a reduced risk of

17. Dancing and the brain article Harvard Medical School 2015.

dementia. A study by researchers at the Albert Einstein College of Medicine[18] found that dancing is associated with 76 per cent reduced risk of dementia among the participants.

Another study published in the Frontiers in Aging Neuroscience[19] showed that dancing improves cognitive health by improving one of the cognitive areas known as spatial memory.

The study also suggests that maintaining an active lifestyle into old age can preserve motor and perceptual abilities.

Salsa dancing

Having experimented with many dancing styles over the years, I have developed a love for Latin American dance styles, especially salsa. Dance has been a way for me to incorporate exercise into my life, both at the gym and when I'm running training workshops for my clients. Where possible, I incorporate singing and dancing into my workshops to help improve cognitive function.

A study carried out by Coventry University[20] academics for BBC One's The Truth About Getting Fit 2018 suggests that salsa dancing can boost brain function.

The results showed an improvement in the three areas of brain function tested. This included coincidence anticipation, which is the ability to respond to a moving stimulus such as catching a ball and visual discrimination, which is how fast and accurately people respond to particular symbols or visual cues.

But the researchers' biggest surprise in the third area was how much the dancer's visual-spatial working memory improved after the period of salsa dancing. Visual spatial working memory is the ability to hold visual information within the brain and then replicate it.

18. The New England Journal of Medicine 2002 - Leisure Activities and the Risk of Dementia in the Elderly & New Medical Life Sciences 'Is dancing good for the brain' article 2019.   19. Frontiers in Aging Neuroscience, Clinical trial article 2016.   20. Coventry University re: Salsa Dancing research article 2018.

The test showed an average improvement of 18 per cent after the salsa dancing, compared to improvements of between five and 10 per cent for the other areas of cognitive function tested.

Sleep and the brain

When clients mention how exhausted they are feeling and I review how they are setting up their brain and body for success throughout their week, many are not getting enough quality sleep and waking up with a less than ideal battery charge. I often ask the question, "What do you do before going to sleep?"

Using IT devices directly before going to sleep can stimulate your brain. My client, Emy, was unable to fall asleep quickly and liked to reward herself at the end of a busy day by playing games on her device directly before going to bed. This was stimulating her brain and stopping her from switching off.

Relaxing, light stretching and dimming the lights before bed can help tap into melatonin, the hormone that helps us feel sleepy and fall asleep. For me, stretching and listening to a sleep meditation helps me fall asleep in a relaxed state without my brain thinking of all the things I need to do (that used to be me).

In some of my peak mental performance workshops, attendees often say they need to increase the amount of sleep by a number of hours per night, but this can actually make you feel worse. If your goal is to increase the amount of sleep, start increasing it by 15 to 30 mins over two weeks, before increasing it further. Observe how you feel over the two-weeks because otherwise you will experience symptoms like jet lag throughout your day.

Let me introduce you to Lisa Maltman, the founder of The Sleep Connection. We met in Sydney a few years ago when we attended each other's keynote at a school education program. I love the work Lisa does and asked her to share some key insights.

Lisa Maltman - founder of The Sleep Connection

Why is sleep so important?

We sleep for approximately one-third of our lives. The quality of our sleep influences the quality of the two-thirds of our time spent awake.

Sleep impacts our health, resilience and performance

Sleep impacts just about every area of our physical health including our immunity, cardiovascular system, blood sugar control, metabolism and weight gain and reproductive system, and is even linked to brain diseases such as Alzheimer's.

Sleep impacts our desire to exercise and, for those elite athletes out there, it plays a major role in improving athletic performance and competitive results.

Sleep also affects physical growth and brain development in our children.

Mental health and resilience

Poor sleep can lead to negative patterns of thinking and emotional vulnerability. This can negatively impact relationships and overall mood, and can be associated with depression, anxiety, negative body image and low self-esteem.

Sleep also impacts on our stress hormones. By getting the sleep we need, our stress levels are lowered, and we are less likely to become overwhelmed. We have a more positive outlook on life and respond better to challenges life throws us.

Additionally, a lack of sleep influences our children's behaviour and sometimes can be associated with behavioural challenges like attention deficit hyperactivity disorder (ADHD – a neurodevelopmental disorder characterised by inattention, or excessive activity and impulsivity).

Sleep directly affects our motivation

The quality and amount of sleep you get regularly affects your cognitive sharpness, productivity, motivation and decision-making capacity.

In our children, these effects impact their focus at school and learning outcomes.

A guide to hours of sleep per night

Different people have different sleep needs to function at their best. The Sleep Health Foundation – Australia's Leading Advocate for Healthy Sleep[21] suggests the times in the table below as a guide. You can make a good guess if a person is sleeping enough at night - observe how they act and function during the day.

Age	Hours per night
Preschoolers (three – five years old)	10 – 13 hours
School-aged children (six – 13 years old)	9 – 11 hours
Teens (14 – 17 years old)	8 – 10 hours
Adult (18 – 64 years old)	7 – 9 hours

21. The Sleep Health Foundation – Australia's Leading Advocate for Healthy Sleep, with information on most sleep topics www.sleephealthfoundation.org.au/fact-sheets.html

Ten Tips for improving your sleep:

1. **Prioritise your sleep and create a consistent sleep schedule**

2. **Keep your bedroom for sleep and sex only (so your brain makes these associations).**

3. **Set a digital curfew one to two hours prior to sleep time and keep devices out of your bedroom at night. This is key due to the four ways digital devices may compromise your sleep:**

    A) It's easy for devices to cause users to displace more sleep time than they're aware of;

    B) The arousal effect of technology causes an increase in physical and mental arousal / stimulation. Even the mere presence of devices in your room may have an effect;

    C) The blue light emitted from screens impacts our sleepy hormone, melatonin, in the brain. For some people this can make it harder to fall asleep and or have a good quality deep sleep;

    D) Alerts and notifications lead to interrupted sleep cycles.

4. **Avoid alcohol right before bed**

Alcohol disrupts circadian rhythms and reduces sleep quality.

5. **Avoid caffeine and other stimulants in the afternoon**

Caffeine affects everyone differently. According to the American Academy of Sleep Medicine, caffeine's half-life is up to five hours. Half-life is the amount of time it takes for a quantity of a substance to be reduced to half the original amount. Even the remaining half can continue to impact some people's ability to fall asleep and / or have a good quality sleep.

6. Exercise regularly and eat well

Exercise increases the time the body spends in deep sleep, which is the most physically restorative sleep phase. When and what you eat can also impact your sleep quality.

7. Implement a wind-down period / or stress reduction techniques

Mindfulness and deep breathing are techniques to assist people falling asleep and allow them to experience better quality sleep. Apps like Smiling Minds, Headspace and Calm have guided sleep programs.

8. Set aside thinking and planning time – keep a pen and paper beside your bed

Write down any challenges or concerns you have well before bedtime, including potential solutions for these. This will reduce rumination in the middle of the night. Having a pen and paper beside your bed means you can quickly write down anything that comes to mind and forget about it until when you awake in the morning.

9. Keep naps to 20 minutes only and not too late in the afternoon

Twenty minutes or less gives you a power nap whilst staying in your light sleep cycle. Any longer and you start to enter into a deep sleep and waking from deep sleep rather than light sleep can leave you feeling groggy.

10. Keep a sleep diary

Complete a two-week sleep diary. This will start to give you a picture of your sleep health and help you to be aware of the appropriate steps to improve your sleep.

If you have children, have them join you in keeping a sleep diary and ensure sleep is prioritised for the whole family. Dr Chris Seton, a key adolescent and paediatric sleep specialist from the Woolcock Institute of Medical Research, believes that 70 per cent of teens are sleep deprived, which can lead to serious consequences.

 **Just do it:**

Plan of action / questions to ask yourself:
- Do you feel you get enough sleep?
- If not, what are the main reasons you are not getting the sleep you need?
- How does this impact you?
- What would motivate you to improve your sleep?
- What are the one or two tips you could implement today?

Lastly, act now and seek help if you are concerned about the sleep health of you and / or your family members – see reference section on where to get professional help if required.

Lisa Maltman is Founder of The Sleep Connection. If you are interested in running a Corporate, Community or School Program, then please contact her via:
lisa@thesleepconnection.com.au

....

The importance of social connection

Humans are born to connect, regardless of whether we have introverted or extroverted personalities. It is more than just physical needs, we are emotionally, cognitively, and spiritually hardwired for

connection, love, and belonging. Connection, along with love and belonging, is why we are here, and it is what gives purpose and meaning to our lives. The brain is often referred to as a social organ.

In the first six months of our life, the right brain hemisphere growth relies on facial expression, tone of voice, gestures, eye contact and timing, gauging the intensity of a response. We have a biological need for human interaction.

We have different mental maps, as no two brains are the same. And yet, we often assume we are on the same page as other people and that the information in your brain is known to others. If only I had a dollar for every time a person says to me, "Why are people so stupid?" My response is, "What may seem common knowledge or rational thinking to you is based on your experiences, beliefs and learnings. Every person's journey, no matter how similar, is different."

Therefore, communication is one of the toughest skills to master, as we all interpret things differently. We could look at our favourite painting or hear our favourite song and give it a different meaning to another.

The effects of social pain

The brain's social pain system may have piggybacked onto the physical pain system during mammalian evolution, borrowing the pain signal to indicate broken social bonds[22]. Although people generally agree that our basic survival needs are food, water and shelter, because mammalian young are born immature and incapable of providing for their own physical needs, they must stay connected to their caregivers. In young mammals, the need for this social connection supersedes the need for food, water and shelter, because without a caregiver

22. Eisenberger & Lieberman, 2004; Panksepp, 1998.

to provide for these needs, young mammals would not survive. Just as evolution has wired us to feel pain when we lack food (e.g. hunger), water (e.g. thirst), or shelter (e.g. freezing, sunburn), perhaps evolution has wired us to feel pain when we lack or anticipate a lack of social connection.

Just as we have primary needs necessary for our survival, we now understand that the brain also treats social needs as primary needs, and when they are not met we can experience a strong threat response.

Neuroscientists have discovered that the same regions of the brain are activated when we experience physical and social pain. What we understand from this is that a threat to one's status is experienced by the brain as acutely as a threat to one's life. Social pain hurts![23]

Clearly, it is important to understand the brain is a social organ, and emotional pain affects our brain in a similar way to physical pain. If we sense a social connection threat, such as being ignored by our boss or a member of our team, we can try and suppress this or ignore it, but that is not the way the brain works.

When we sense this threat, our limbic system (the emotional centre) becomes activated to keep us safe and minimise the danger. Understanding the brain as a social organ is one of the keys to being a good connector, leader and communicator, regardless of whether you are an introvert or extrovert personality.

Dr Matthew Lieberman and Dr Naomi Eisenberger (husband and wife team) have been investigating social pain. They have undertaken some fascinating research that shows that some of the same neural regions that we see active when we experience physical pain are also active when we experience social pain. In the references section, you can review the video clip, which explains the notion that social pain hurts.

23. Dr Matthew Lieberman and Dr Naomi Eisenberger – Watch YouTube video www.youtube.com/watch?v=X7EFYwUopf8 4:38 mins – April 2010.

In summary, Eisenberger says, "We see there are connections between certain personality traits and how sensitive people are to both physical pain and social rejection. People who tend to be more neurotic or anxious are more sensitive to physical pain and more easily distressed by rejection. Extroverts are less sensitive to physical pain and also seem to be less distressed by social rejection."

Gratitude

Gratitude is strongly and consistently associated with greater happiness. Gratitude helps people feel more positive emotions, relish good experiences, improve their health, deal with adversity and build strong connections.

When we express gratitude and receive the same, our brain releases dopamine and serotonin, the two crucial neurotransmitters responsible for our emotions, and they make us feel 'good'. They enhance our mood immediately.

When you feel grateful, you experience synchronised activation of many parts of your brain, giving you positive effects. Some of my clients and I have incorporated gratefulness into our weekly way of life for a few key reasons; it allows us to reflect on what's important to us and it will enable the good things in our lives to shine bright, regardless of how the day turned out. It allows us to be present and enjoy the positive things in our busy day without them being lost.

Another benefit of sharing your gratitude with others is that it helps you to connect with and appreciate others, you can stimulate the release of dopamine in someone else (the brain's happy natural feel-good drug).

One of my clients is a human resources manager for a department in Queensland Health. She was printing important information

in preparation for a critical board meeting when the printer stopped working, just moments before the meeting.
She was experiencing a high threat state when a person walking past offered to help by fixing the problem. My client found herself running down the corridor to be at the meeting on time and prepared in front of senior management, feeling so relieved.

Reflecting that night, the HR Manager reviewed her day and felt very grateful for her colleague's help. The next day she shared her appreciation, and at first, the colleague dismissed it, as he didn't think he added much value. He down-played it by saying, "Oh, it was nothing, happy to help." The HR Manager expressed how much it meant and explained the ramifications for this important meeting, so the recipient felt great, and a relationship connection was strengthened.

COVID was a time when I saw people be grateful for things like having flexible hours and working from home. I recall going to our favourite café for the first time after the first round of COVID restrictions eased and seeing one of the workers, India, and noticing her beaming smile. I commented on her amazing smile, and she replied as she bounced around the tables, "I am so delighted to be working again. I didn't realise how much I missed seeing customers and staff members."

During a recent online high-performance training program, one of the attendees shared how grateful she was to be working and have flexible options working from home. In general, people seem to be valuing autonomy and choice.

Tips for putting gratitude into your weekly or daily routine

There are many ways to implement gratitude. I tend to reflect at night before going to sleep but have clients that do it morning, lunchtime and evening. The following is a guideline.

 **Just do it:**

Identify how you could make gratitude part of your routine and how often.

Morning
Three things I am grateful for: ➔ ➔ ➔
Three things that would make today great: ➔ ➔ ➔
Three daily affirmations. I am: ➔ ➔ ➔
Evening
Three amazing things that happened today: ➔ ➔ ➔
Three things that could have made today better: ➔ ➔ ➔

Social connectedness

Clinical Psychologist, Dr Marta Miller, has spent most of her working life working with adults and older adults who experience mental health disorders or significant physical health injuries / illnesses.

Marta and I have known each other for over 20 years and have a mutual passion for observing human behaviour. We have spent many nights talking over dinner and into the early hours of the morning. I have asked her to share her insights on the importance of social connectedness and some of the research she has come across.

Dr Marta Miller – Clinical Psychologist

The importance of social connection

Experiencing a sense of social connectedness is essential for most people as it involves the social interactions that people have with others and the sense of belonging a person feels. Social connectedness is about the individual and personal bonds that is felt and experienced.

The sense of social connection that people have with those around them appears to influence how and when they make major life decisions, such as where to live, what activities are engaged in or even deciding when to retire from work. Regarding work, it has been found that workers who spend their free time more engaged with family and friends often retire earlier from work than those who spend their spare time occupied with work matters and connections. These latter individuals tended to choose to work longer and retire at an older age in comparison to people who experience a personal sense of connection with others. This suggests that workers receive diverse benefits from the different types of social connections they experience, which can influence their decision about when to shift from employment to retirement.[24]

Social connection is not only influenced by work, but it is also related to age. It appears that the older adults become, the

24. Lancee and Radl 2012.

more content they are with the relationships they do have, as loneliness seems to steadily decrease as people mature. More than 60 per cent of young adults (18 to 22 years) have been found to experience feelings of loneliness compared to 18 to 30 per cent of people over 72 years of age.[25]

Not all types of social support and social connection can be viewed as beneficial, however. There are instances where too much support or identifying too much with a group can be detrimental. Examples that have been observed are connections with people who erode a person's sense of self-efficacy and confidence or following a group to 'fit in', especially if it is against a person's better judgement or competing values. In other words, not all social connections or relationships are protective factors, and it is the supportive protective connections that should be sought out. Social connectedness is more than just the number of people we talk to or know in a day.

In a recent study of 20,000 American adults, 54 per cent of participants reported they experienced a sense of loneliness as they ranged from 'sometimes' to 'always' feeling as if no one knew them, while 47 per cent of people indicated they often felt left out of social networks. The study went on to report that thirty-nine per cent of participants stated they no longer felt socially or emotionally close to anyone with a further 43 per cent revealing that the relationships do they have with others are not meaningful. Social connectedness and relationships are viewed as so important and necessary for people to live a fulfilling life that Martin Seligman, a pioneer in positive psychology, posited it as being one of the core pillars that needs to be addressed for people to achieve a state of wellbeing and happiness.

25. Cigna & Ipsos, 2018.

Some tips to enhance your social connectedness with others.

→ Say hello and smile at people around you throughout your day

→ Make the time to participate in forming a new social relationship

→ Enhance an existing relationship by going for a walk with someone

→ Join a group at the local community centre (have a shared interest with others)

→ Offer to do something kind for someone who needs a bit of help (e.g. run an errand for an elderly neighbour)

→ Spend time being mindful of the moment when you are engaging with others rather than thinking about other things.

The impact of social connection on health

Forty-two per cent of people who do not experience their relationships as meaningful are more likely to be suffering from adequate to poor health in comparison to 12 per cent of adults who are satisfied with their social connectedness.

For decades, researchers have shown the relationship between social connection and health or length of life. A longitudinal study conducted in America found that the more connected people feel with their family, friends, and community, the longer they live in comparison to individuals who have the least connections.[26] The results were similar for both men and women between 30 and 69 years of age. The importance of

26. Berkman and Syme, 1979.

social relationships was demonstrated, even when factors such as health problems, disability, obesity, smoking, drinking, etc. and socioeconomic status were controlled for. The correlation between early mortality and having low social connection continued to be seen, with people who experienced the fewest relationships at significantly greater risk of dying early.

Research in Japan[27], England[28], and Australia[29] have shown similar results; people who have more significant social connection with others tend to live longer than those who do not. This finding was further supported by a meta-analysis review[30] of 148 studies from around the world, involving almost 309,000 participants. This showed a 50 per cent increased probability of a longer life span for people if they had stronger sense of social connection with others.

Social connectedness has also been found to be associated with cardiac risk factors. More socially isolated people experience a greater chance of developing elevated levels of fibrinogen, which is a blood plasma protein and is a risk factor for cardiac concerns when the level is too high[31]. Even after adjusting for known cardiac risk factors, such as age, sex and level of education, people experiencing less social connection continued to be at greater risk of developing potential cardiac issues.

The impact of social connection on mental health

People who have increased levels of social connectedness generally experience better mental health while those who have few social connections were at increased risk of developing or experiencing mental health problems such as depression[32], post-traumatic stress[33] or suicidal ideation[34].

27. Sugisawa, Liang & Liu, 1994. 28. Bennett, 2002. 29. Giles, Glonek, Luszcz & Andrews, 2005.
30. Holt-Lunstad, Smith & Layton, 2010. 31. Kim, Benjamin, Fowler & Christakis, 2016. 32. Cruwys, Dingle, Haslam, et al., 2013; Czyz, Liu & King, 2012. 33. Kintzle, Barr, Corletto & Castro, 2018. 34. Czyz, Liu & King, 2012; Fanning & Pietrzakab, 2013; Reyes et al., 2020.

In Australia, about 6 out of 10 men aged between 30 and 65 years of age have revealed they experience low levels of depression and / or anxiety at some point in their life while seventeen per cent of men indicated their levels of depression and anxiety have been very high[35]. Men who suffered from very high levels of emotional distress reported having poor social support whereas men who experienced low psychological distress reported having strong social connections.

Experiencing a sense of belonging and a social connection with others is an important protective factor for people's heath; both physically and mentally. Developing meaningful relationships with others is essential for improving and maintaining good emotional and physical health as well as enhancing the quality of life that is experienced.

Impact of a pandemic like COVID-19

During the COVID-19 pandemic, several mental health agencies (e.g. Beyond Blue, Lifeline) as well as Australian government representatives have reported a substantial increase in the number of people accessing mental health support via helplines and services. A number of factors are thought to have contributed to this increased need for support, including isolation and the loss of social connection experienced[36]. The paucity of feeling connected with others has led to an increase in psychological distress being experienced.

I saw the impact that restrictions and the resulting social isolation had on many people during COVID-19 through family, friends, colleagues, clients and carers. Many individuals who had never experienced a mental illness previously or hadn't come to the attention of mental health services before, were for the first time reaching out to professionals for emotional

35. Hall & Partners, 2014.   36. Smith & Lim, 2020.

support. Predominantly, most became depressed with some experiencing thoughts of suicide.

During the pandemic in Australia, telehealth was promoted and widely utilised by many service providers, including mental health providers. This was in an effort to ensure the safety of professionals and clients alike and to reduce the risk of potential exposure to the virus by minimising the amount of interactions needing to take place person to person. Although telehealth was effective for many, in my opinion, it was not suitable for all. Some individuals found telehealth failed to meet their needs as they still felt cut-off or remote from clinicians. Some individuals found looking at a clinician through a computer or mobile phone screen acted as a barrier. They ended up feeling even more alone because they no longer saw their friends and / or family face-to-face and no longer saw professionals either. Some clients reported they felt abandoned by everyone as they had no-one left with whom they were interacting. Some people reported they missed the simple act of kindness of when the clinician handed them a box of tissues when they cried. Although telehealth was and will likely continue to be an effective avenue for the majority of clients who require support to manage their psychological distress, it will not be suitable for everyone.

While this topic is about the importance of social connectedness, it was interesting to observe that not everyone responded poorly to social isolation or felt a sense of social disconnection during COVID-19. There were some individuals, such as those with germ or social phobias, who seemed to respond well to the restrictions and reported they were 'thrilled' that they would no longer be expected to shake people's hands, to hug others, or be questioned when they declined to attend group activities or give public talks. While this may have been the experience for a few, others were content to try and get on with their life to the best of their ability and yet many others really struggled with the loss of being socially connected.

Some tips for social connection during times of change include:

- Make or receive telephone calls. Ensure that people who need contact regularly, hear your voice. Let people know you care about them and are thinking of them; that they are not forgotten.

- Use platforms such as Zoom, facetime, what's app, etc. to speak with friends and family so that you can see them as well as hear them.

- Focus on people who are more in need than yourself – e.g. Ask elderly neighbours or those with disabilities if you can get their groceries for them. If you have skills or some spare time do things for others who cannot financially afford practical help such as mow someone else's lawn, do their gardening, fix their squeaky gate, repair their leaky tap, knit blankets for people who are homeless, cook a meal for someone in need, etc.

- Join online groups with similar interests to you. You will automatically have something in common with everyone else in the group.

- Join a volunteer group where social distancing can be maintained, e.g. bush regeneration, removing graffiti, caring for injured wildlife, reciting books or poems on digital / audio platforms for people to listen to who are visually impaired, etc. Many places need your time or your labour rather than just your money.

- Reconnect with old friends and acquaintances. Let them know you had been thinking of them and wanted to know how they were.

- Change your perspective – e.g. use strategies from cognitive behavioural therapy or acceptance and commitment therapy to change the way you think about or perceive things.

- Join a club or take up a sporting activity.

- Host a morning tea and invite a few neighbours over to get to know them better.

- Study something that interests you and keep learning. Learning stimulates the brain and creates new neural connections.

The benefits of and options to mindfulness

You may have heard of mindfulness. It is the quality of being present and fully engaged with whatever we are doing at the moment. But what exactly is mindfulness, and how can you recognise it and reap its many benefits? According to mindful research, the practice can have numerous benefits, including decreased stress and sadness levels and increased focus and happiness.

Studies have found that regular meditation practice increases the protein brain-derived neurotrophic factor (BDNF) in the brain, improves cellular health, reduces the rate of aging within cells, and reduces grey matter[37] decay in the brain, making it possible for increased levels of neuroplasticity over extended periods of time.

Mindfulness is a type of meditation in which you focus on being intensely aware of what you're sensing and feeling in the moment, without interpretation or judgment. Practising mindfulness involves using breathing methods, guided imagery, and other practices to relax the body and mind and help reduce stress. When stress, anxiety, or sleepless nights leave you feeling deflated, increasing your oxygen throughout your day using mindfulness practices can help you bounce back to your natural, happy state.

My mindfulness journey and that of some of my clients has been an interesting exploration. Initially, some people think it is impossible for them to stop thinking and detach from their thoughts, but I have found it to be a crucial skill. It has taken me plenty of trial and error to find what is right for me, and I'm still exploring options. I have become passionate about providing my clients with a wide range of alternatives, depending on their needs, desired outcomes and environment.

A number of my clients have found mindfulness practices useful to either set up their day or to separate work, study and personal life, especially with working from home, and to help with unwinding from a busy day, which I refer to as changing gears within the brain. It also helps with building resilience to obstacles and challenges that arise.

Mindfulness meditation practice is one way to experience the current moment and integrate that awareness into your everyday life. Here are a few options for you to explore and get started.

---

37. Wikipedia – Grey matter contains most of the brain's neuronal cell bodies. The grey matter includes regions of the brain involved in muscle control, and sensory perception such as seeing and hearing, memory, emotions, speech, decision making, and self-control.

Meditation apps

There are a number of meditation options available, and busy professionals juggling many things in their lives may prefer the convenience of using a meditation app. This provides a resource at our fingertips, one that can fit in with our schedules, be used as a brain break in between meetings, or set an intention or goal. It can help extend our brain's capacity within a day.

Here are some mindfulness, sleep and music program options that my clients and I have explored and found effective:

Breethe app - www.breethe.com

Headspace - www.headspace.com/mindfulness

Smiling Minds – www.smilingmind.com.au

Calm - www.calm.com

One of my favourite mindfulness 'Letting go' series learnings is on the Breethe app.

There are specific ways that we can choose to react to challenging situations that create stress. Between our brain's stimulus and response, there is a space. In that space is our power to choose our response. In our response lies our possible growth and our freedom. What does this mean?

When we live in a fight, flight, freeze mode, like most of us do, we react automatically to whatever triggers us. It happens so quickly that we don't choose our reaction. As we bring awareness to these moments, the process opens up a bit, and a tiny space is created in which we can consciously choose our response. In that space, we can choose to let go.

Letting go means full acceptance and full release. It's not about the suppression of feelings. When we suppress what we are experiencing, we are planting the seeds of future resentment. 'Letting go' is one of the most powerful skills we can practise to gain greater peace in our lives.

We can let go of the behaviours that create our stress, and of the need to be right, which creates conflict. We can let go of grudges and grievances that keep us feeling resentful and angry. We can let go of thought patterns that keep us stuck and inhibit our growth. Meditation provides an opportunity to practise letting go.

Ajahn Chah says, "If you let go a little you will have a little peace; if you let go a lot you will have a lot of peace; if you let go completely you will have complete peace".

According to Eckhart Tolle, author of The Power of Now, we create our problems because they give us a sense of identity. This may explain why we tend to hold onto our pain far beyond its ability to serve us. We continuously replay past mistakes in our heads, allowing feelings of shame and regret to shape our actions in the present. We cling to frustrations and worry about the future as if we have control over it. We hold stress and anger in our minds and bodies, potentially causing serious health issues. We accept that the resulting anxiety as a natural state. Life may not be totally simple, but there is always time to practise accepting life. Every moment is a chance to let go and be peaceful and kind.

Some of my other favourite quotes by Eckhart Tolle: *"The past has no power over the present moment"*; *"Some changes look negative on the surface, but you will soon realise that space is being created in your life for something new to emerge"*; *"The primary cause of unhappiness is never the situation but your thoughts about it"*.

Being calm under pressure

Increasing your oxygen throughout your day is key to being calm under pressure and we will explore the why and the how throughout this section.

Leveraging breathing apps on devices like an Apple Watch or Fitbit can help remind you to increase your oxygen even for one or two minutes between meetings or calls. If you start to feel overwhelmed, simply tap and start breathing, only focussing on your breath going in and out deeply.

Beyond stress and anxiety relief, deep breathing also helps lower blood pressure, reduces lactic acid build-up (which occurs when there's not enough oxygen in the muscles), boosts the immune system, enhances focus, and improves the retention of new information.

Breathwork

Breathwork, a tool that has been used in ancient cultures for thousands of years, is now gaining more and more traction in the modern world. And for good reasons.

The act of breathing is an autonomic behaviour just like the pumping of the heart. Breathing is a function of the Autonomic Nervous System (ANS) and does not require conscious thinking for it to occur.

However, it can be consciously manipulated and controlled to significantly improve mental cognition and performance, lower emotional reactivity as well as improving overall health and wellbeing.

Changing patterns of breathing allows you to change your stress response in relation to environmental conditions and patterns of thinking which occur both consciously and unconsciously.

Breathwork can be used as a tool to switch between the sympathetic and parasympathetic nervous systems[38] within the body.

Breathwork is now more accessible and more accepted as a tool for personal development and improved performance by the western world.

My friend Rachelle introduced me to a breath work expert, Daniel Garbett, owner of Feel Alive, and together we've enjoyed the benefits of his breath work apps. I have asked Daniel to contribute his knowledge.

....

Daniel Garbett – Owner of Feel Alive

Breathing is our doorway to understanding the connection between the mind and the body, there is a link between the pattern of your breathing and the emotional responses within your body. To understand this, you need to know that within your lungs there are receptor sites which monitor the speed, volume, and rate of your breathing patterns. These messages travel to your emotional centre within your brain, influencing the emotions and thought patterns that you experience.

What's important to note is that this response also works in opposite direction, meaning that your thoughts and emotions can also influence the pattern of your breathing. Your sympathetic nervous system (fight / flight / freeze) is activated by the perception of stress within your environment which changes your breathing pattern, meaning that your perception can influence your breathing pattern.

Your unconscious mind becomes conditioned over time to

---

38. Wikipedia – The autonomic nervous system comprises two parts – the sympathetic and parasympathetic nervous system. The sympathetic nervous system activates the fight, flight or freeze response during a threat or perceived danger, and the parasympathetic nervous system restores the body to a state of calm.

respond to situations in the environment in a specific way, if your default response to these events in your environment trigger your 'stress response,' you will unconsciously develop breathing patterns reflecting a stressful state. This occurs even if there is no 'physical stress' in the environment and can lead to chronic low-level stress which shows up as burn out, irritability, brain fog, agitation, and other adverse health conditions.

When you become conscious of your breath in moments of stress or when in an undesired state during your day, breathe in a way that triggers your parasympathetic nervous system to come back online. Slow deep breathing in moments of stress can break old psychological patterns and provides you with a way of regulating your energy and state in response to stress.

Two things you need to know:

1) Slowing down your breathing will activate your parasympathetic nervous system (rest / relax / restore)

2) Taking a deep breath in followed by a big 'sigh' will trigger relaxation

So, when you want to begin reconditioning your breathing patterns, incorporate conscious breathing practices at regular intervals throughout your day.

Shamanic breathing:

One of my favourite breath practices is Shamanic Circular Breathing. As previously mentioned, many cultures have used breathwork for thousands of years as a self-development and growth tool because it allows us to access altered states of consciousness. This specific breathing practice can trigger the release of different hormones and neurotransmitters within the body, which enables us to access altered states, and release tension and emotion stored within the body. It is known by many as transformational breathing because you transcend your physical body, move beyond your identity and have a transcendental experience. This practice is all about 'letting go'; letting go of judgments, letting go of resistance, letting go of attachments and moving into a state of acceptance. This practice is highly experiential, and each individual's inner experience brings healing, wisdom and a deep connection to self.

I talk about the process of shamanic breathing more in depth and teach you how you can explore shamanic breathing as a self-development tool in the Coherent Breathwork App[39]. However, to give you a taste of shamanic breathing, you can follow the steps below:

1) Find yourself a quiet, comfortable space to lie

2) Put on your favourite meditation music and close your eyes

3) Completely relax your body

4) Begin breathing deeply in through your nose for the count of 3 seconds and out through your mouth for the count of 3 seconds

5) Breath continuously and never hold your breath

6) Continue for as long as you would like

7) Slow your breathing down, if at any point, the experience becomes too intense for you.

Again, this is just a place to start with shamanic breathing. In the Coherent Breathwork App, there are guided sessions and video tutorials to give you a better understanding of this specific practice as well as the stages that you can move through in this practice.

39. www.feel-alive.com.au/breathwork

One key thing to be aware of throughout this specific breath practice is you may experience what we call 'tetany'.
This comes from the Greek word 'tetanos' meaning 'convulsive tension'.

Parts of your body may feel stiff and cramped, most often experienced in your hands; however, it may also occur in other parts of your body, such as your lips and feet.

From a biological perspective, the change in your blood chemistry is causing temporary involuntary muscular contractions. However, in the breathwork world we experience this as a deep somatic experience often followed by a release of psychological or physical trauma.

If you do experience these involuntary muscular contractions, it is important to acknowledge that it is there, don't fight it and practise the act of 'letting go'.

1) Non-Judgement

2) Non-Reaction

3) Non-Attachment

Understand the sensation is occurring and continue bringing your awareness to your breath. Once your session is over, the sensation leaves your body relatively quick.

The Coherent Breathwork App

The Coherent Breathwork App was created to bring together everything you need to know to lower chronic low grade stress and improve health through breathwork therapy. As well, it teaches you how to incorporate powerful breath practices into your life as a tool for self-discovery, self-development, and improved performance.

The Coherent Breathwork App is a series of videos which explain what breath work is, why it is so important and how it can improve your life. The app includes a series of breath work practices that can be used for relaxation, inner peace, focus, transformation, improved performance and much more. Each practice comes with guided video sessions which you can carry in your pocket and access whenever you need.

Daniel Garbett, Owner of Feel Alive
wwww.feel-alive.com.au/breathwork

....

 **Just do it:**

Schedule breaks in your diary between meetings to help rejuvenate your body and brain via breathing mindfully.

Yoga

Yoga is a physical practice of mindfulness and detachment. Over the years, I experimented with different types of yoga until I experienced remarkable results with Nivriti Gargya, founder and senior teacher at Mystique Moksha Yoga Studio. Every week, I look forward to Nivriti's Saturday morning yoga class. It frees me by releasing the tension accumulated from the week's exercise, work and daily life from my body and mind. When we chant as a group, I experience the vibrations of the whole group, and the experience feels like we are on the movie set of Avatar connecting to a higher energy source (tribe-like).

When I walk out of Nivriti's yoga class, I feel a lightness, freedom and pure joy. I practise a set of yoga moves most mornings to help set up my focus and intention for the day. I have asked Nivriti to share some of her valuable yoga insights.

Nivriti Gargya – Yoga therapist, Pranic Healer

The relevance of yoga today

Yoga is a science of right living. As such, it needs to be incorporated into our daily lives. It works on all the aspects of a person; the physical, vital, mental, emotional, psychic, and spiritual. While yoga's central theme remains a spiritual journey, regular yoga practice gives people direct and tangible benefits regardless of their spiritual aims. Yoga can be a successful alternative form of therapy. The number of people currently practising yoga is increasing dramatically.

Understanding yoga

The word yoga originated from the Sanskrit word 'YUJ' which means to join / to connect. Joining Jivatman (individual self) to Parmatman (supreme being), it is an expansion of the narrow constricted egoistic personality to an all pervasive, eternal, and blissful state of reality. As per yoga scriptures, we have the five sheaths of the body (Panch Koshas), and when we follow the holistic approach to practising yoga, it benefits us on each level. We start the practice from the outermost level (physical body); however, yoga benefits us from the inside out. Sage Patanjali, who is considered a modern guru of yoga, gave structure to various tools of yoga through his scripture known as PATANJALI YOGA SUTRA. He called them 'ASHTANGA' eight limbs of yoga.

The eight limbs of yoga and the five sheaths are part of our teaching at Mystique Moksha Yoga Studio' and they take the participants on a self-discovery journey.

Nivriti Gargya, Yoga therapist | Pranic Healer
Founder and Senior Teacher, Mystique Moksha Yoga Studio
www.mystiquemoksha.com.au

Music therapy

Music can boost cognition function and connect both hemispheres of the brain, facilitating more effective retrieval of information from each side of the brain. Music also can be a great strategy for relieving stress and reducing a threat response.

On a corporate and individual level, music therapy helps relieve stress and anxiety, improves quality of life, prepares you for an important meeting or presentation and provides mood enhancement.

During my studies of the brain, I was fascinated by how playing a musical instrument benefits your brain.

Did you know that every time musicians pick up their instruments, there are fireworks going off all over their brain? On the outside, they may look calm and focused, reading the music and making the precise and practised movements required, but inside their brains, there is a party going on. How do we know this?

Well, in the last few decades neuroscientists have made enormous breakthroughs in understanding how our brains work by monitoring them in real-time with instruments like functional Magnetic Resonance Imaging (fMRI) scan, a scan that measures and maps the brain's activity) and Positron Emission Tomography (PET) scan, a scan that is a functional imaging technique that uses radioactive substances known as radiotracers to visualise and measure changes in metabolic processes and other physiological activities including blood flow, regional chemical composition, and absorption.

When people are hooked up to these machines, we can observe that different areas of the brain are activated, and which correspond to different tasks, such as reading or doing mathematical problems.

When researchers asked participants to listen to music, they saw fireworks going off in both hemispheres of the brain. In addition, multiple areas of their brain lit up simultaneously as participants processed the sound, took it apart to understand elements like melody and rhythm, and then put it all back together into a unified musical experience. And our brains do all this work in the split second between when we first hear the music and when our foot starts to tap along.

When scientists shifted their attention from observing the brains of music listeners to those of musicians, the little backyard fireworks became a jubilee. It turns out that while listening to music engages the brain in some interesting activities, playing music is the brain's equivalent of a full-body workout. The neuroscientists say multiple areas of the brain light up, simultaneously processing different information in intricate, interrelated and astonishingly fast sequences.

But what is it about making music that sets the brain alight? Playing a musical instrument engages practically every area of the brain at once, especially the visual, auditory, and motor cortices. As with any other workout, disciplined, structured practice of playing music strengthens those brain functions allowing us to apply that strength to other activities like recalling information from both hemispheres of the brain.

The second thing that helps connect information from both hemispheres of the brain effectively is being multilingual – speaking different languages.

 Just do it:

Listening to music can help set the right mood before presenting, being interviewed, or attending an important meeting. It can help energise your brain so you can change gears and recall information. How could you use music in your life?

I introduce you to Nicole Masseque, Co-Founder of Music Therapy for all Ages, who will share valuable insights on how music helps her clients. I have known Nicole for many years, and she has helped many people overcome obstacles in their life through music therapy.

.....

Nicole Masseque – Co-Founder of Music Therapy for all Ages

Music therapy is a therapeutic practice that uses music to address the physical, cognitive, social, and emotional needs of individuals of all ages. Put simply; music therapy helps to significantly improve an individual's quality of life.

Neurological disorders

Although music therapy has been used historically to treat various psychological problems, it was only in the 1980s that empirical research was undertaken in the field.

To date, music therapy has been effective in treating negative psychological symptoms, such as anxiety, stress, and depression.

Neuroplasticity is the brain's ability to change over time with training. It was once believed that at a certain age the brain stopped being able to change and develop. We now know that the brain can continue to develop and change and make new pathways and connections when certain areas are damaged.

Music therapists work with individuals with a variety of neurologic and physical challenges, using the elements of music to make changes in the brain. Music is used to build non-musical goals such as movement, speech, communication, receptive language and cognitive skills.

Music activates various regions of the brain responsible for memory, such as the hippocampus. This means that it can be used therapeutically in patients suffering from neurodegenerative diseases, such as Alzheimer's. Patients' moods can improve, and music can also assist in recalling memories.

How does music therapy work?

Music acts on several parts of the brain, which is why it is so effective in treating stroke and brain injury victims. This is because music can arouse emotions and stimulate social interactions, helping the patient to recover.

Dr Elizabeth Stegemoller, a music therapist with a PhD in neuroscience explores music therapy and neuroplasticity in her article 'Exploring the Mechanisms of Music Therapy'[40].

It is quite challenging to describe what happens in a music therapy session, as there are several treatment approaches.

It can be performed with the patient being passive, just listening to the music therapist playing or a recording. A patient can also be active, where the patient will be making music with the therapist, playing the drums or harp or singing.

For example, I have employed an active treatment approach with a patient who has a severe brain injury. Initially we were using a djembe (African Drum). Our goal was for her to move

---

40. Dr Elizabeth Stegemoller article 'Exploring the Mechanisms of Music Therapy' in The Scientist publication 1st March 2017.

her arms enough to hit the drum, and we also wanted to improve her mood. In a short period of time, she moved her hands to play the drum, she also developed different strategies of how to hit the drum all on her own. Singing during our sessions has also seen her pronounce new words. Six months later, she was observed whistling and singing in tune.

Music therapy sessions are especially useful in helping to develop communication and self-expression skills.

It is also possible for music therapy to be used in groups and for corporate team building activities, where all members play an instrument together and participate in the performance of a song. According to studies, the sessions help participants to relax, feel connected to their peers and express their emotions more easily.

Nicole Masseque. Music therapy for all ages.
www.facebook.com/utchenge

....

The 3 R's - Rest, Recovery and Relaxation

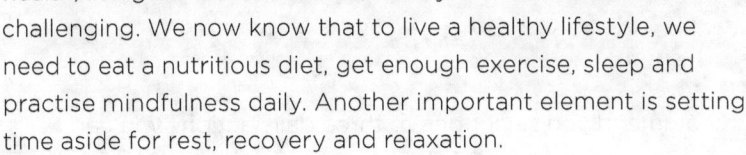

Actioning the previous information about fueling the brain through nurturing your body and mind is one of the most important investments that you can make. Without good health, living our best lives is incredibly challenging. We now know that to live a healthy lifestyle, we need to eat a nutritious diet, get enough exercise, sleep and practise mindfulness daily. Another important element is setting time aside for rest, recovery and relaxation.

Relaxation is often regarded as something we don't have enough time for these days, as we live on a diet of immediacy, of doing more with less. However, relaxing is important, particularly for psychological health. The way we 'relax' means something different to everyone. It might be going for a walk outdoors, practising yoga or meditation or simply sitting quietly and reading a book. Whatever your preference, it should not be overlooked.

Make sure you allocate rest periods, even if you feel like you do not need it. It is important to give your body adequate time to recover, and this is not a one size fits all scenario. It is important from both a physical and psychological standpoint to take the time you need to recover and feel good within. Listen to your body to understand how it is feeling and then recharge. Experiment with different ideas to work out what works best for you in different scenarios and seasons.

For me, a soak in a hot bath with bath salts, candles and listening to Tibetan bell music helps immensely.

Paddle-boarding with my family is also relaxing on a beautiful sunny day; especially when we sit down, put our feet into the water, inhale the smell of the salty fresh air, and admire the stillness of the majestic water around us in the middle of the lake.

My weekly Saturday yoga practice with Nivriti takes me to indescribable places of peace, rest, recovery and relaxation.

 **Just do it:**

What could the 3 R's (Rest, Recovery and Relaxation) look like for you?

I recommend you select one to three daily actions you can focus on over the next 90 days. In my experience, it takes approximately 90 days to create a new habit. Think about the benefits and outcomes this would give you and the impact on those around you.

You know your age, but do you know your brain age? By examining physical changes in the brain associated with advancing age, scientists can assign a number that captures how well your brain functions. A healthy, active 65 year old might have a brain that looks 40 years old. The brain of a 40 year old who is struggling with mental or physical challenges might appear to have the brain of a 65 year old. That hard living 40 year old with the retiree's brain can get back to a place where their cognitive function matches their chronological age by adequately fueling the brain with the right ingredients.

Remember, you control how you fuel your brain and whether you experience benefits like increased cognitive capability, resilience, longer periods of performance, focus, concentration and improved health and well-being.

To conclude this section on 'Fuel your brain with the right ingredients', it may not be possible to do everything on this list and in some cases, you may be doing some of these already. This section is designed to provide you with a buffet of options to explore what is right for you, right now.

SECTION TWO

....

Organise your daily structure based on when you do your best thinking

....

Section Two:

Organise your daily structure based on when you do your best thinking

For decades, work was mostly undertaken in an office and between 9am and 5pm. But then COVID-19 forced us to work remotely, and many people discovered that they could be more productive outside traditional work hours. Others noticed that they were most efficient working in small increments of time. Some people realised that a relaxed environment was conducive to creativity and productivity.

There is an optimal way to work, but when and how you do your best work differs for every person.

Your brain is an organ that needs a large supply of energy throughout the day. On average, you have approximately three hours of productivity within 24 hours from your PFC[41] (Pre-frontal Cortex – executive function of the brain). Using neuroscience strategies, clients have been able to double this, by organising their day around when they do their best thinking.

Over the past decade, we have placed an incredibly high value on immediacy and execution, and we have wrung deep thinking and creativity out of many parts of our professional lives. But the tide is turning. As we head into a future where machines, automation and artificial intelligence (AI) overtake the doing, there has never been a greater premium on deep thinking, innovation, problem solving and creativity.

This section considers the changes in working remotely or a hybrid model of working and the key ingredients for peak performance and productivity.

Key topics covered:

- → Where and when you do your best thinking
- → Productivity tips for setting your brain up for success – reflection on what is working and not working
- → The importance of how you spend your time – using the Pomodoro technique (25 minutes of work and five-minute brain breaks)
- → Build in time for miscellaneous / opportunities that may arise.

---

41. Korn Ferry survey 13 November, 2019. www.kornferry.com/about-us//press/working-or-wasting-time Los Angeles, Nov. 13, 2019.   www.codebots.com/library/way-of-working/how-many-hours-a-day-are-workers-productive   www.cnbc.com/2019/11/17/67percent-of-workers-say-spending-too-much-time-in-meetings-distracts-them.html

Time is precious. How you spend it *matters.*

For the remote or hybrid worker, telecommuting's pros and cons are the opposite sides of the same coin. For some people, the flexible and distraction-free surroundings can become an isolated and demotivating environment. During COVID, parents had the gift of increased family time, but also the added stress of looking after children and their schooling – tasks that would typically be undertaken by professional educators at school.

Without a commitment to both discipline and self-care, workers run the risk of burning out. The Asana Anatomy of work index 2021[42] reported almost 8 in 10 (77%) employees in Australia and New Zealand experienced burnout at least once in the past year – above the global average of 71%. The top factors fueling burnout, according to workers, are: 50% being overloaded; 34% not being able to switch-off / disconnect; and 31% not feeling connected to / supported by their team. The result of burnout has direct business impact on lower morale, more mistakes, lack of engagement, miscommunication and people leaving the company.

As burnout rises, individual engagement levels fall, making work more challenging and impacting organisational resilience as a whole. This can leave workers feeling trapped in groundhog day, becoming discouraged and even depressed.

We are typically more productive and in a 'reward' state when:

→ we know the purpose of what we're working towards

→ we know how we're contributing to the purpose

→ we have identified the outcomes we want to achieve within a time frame

---

42. Asana Anatomy of Work Index 2021. Accessed from: www.asana.com/resources/anatomy-of-work In October 2020, quantitative research was conducted by Sapio Research on behalf of Asana, to understand how people spend time at work.

- we have regular check-ins with our manager, mentor or coach because the goalposts may need to be tweaked as the environment changes
- we have conversations that focus on contribution, not performance (the word performance can throw people into a threat state).

Here are some important ingredients to help you get the most out of your time and effort.

Daily routine check-in

The word 'routine' can send a shudder down some people's spines. It may be perceived as a strict day with no room for fun, free time, or spontaneity. And yet there are so many benefits of a daily routine.

In fact, life can even be easier and more fun once you get yourself on a good schedule that has flexibility and adaptability built in. Take a second to imagine what your workday would be like if there was no routine — no rules, nothing expected of you, no set hours to be there. That might sound fun, but in reality, it may be chaos. Take a moment to imagine what your workday would look like if you applied these three steps.

1. **Identify a new habit**

    Review a habit that no longer serves you and replace it with a new habit for the next 90 days. The key to embedding a new habit is repetition and building in daily reflection time to review what is working and whether there is any opportunity to do it differently to achieve your goal more effectively.

2. **Set a daily intention and visualise the day ahead**

   Setting the intention helps create a great day. Release any negative expectations about the day ahead and decide in this moment how you want to feel and what you want to experience. Visualise what you want to achieve by thinking about who you want to be today. See yourself navigating the day regardless of the obstacles you may face.

3. **Allocate time for the unknown**

   One of my favourite sayings from the Forest Gump movie is, 'Life is like a box of chocolates. You never know what you are going to get'[43]. More than ever, I feel this is true, and I advise busy professionals to allocate time throughout their day, around their key priorities, for the unknown. This allows agility and flexibility; to change and respond to an unexpected request or things that pop up urgently.

   In my experience, most plans don't go the way we initially envisage and being able to adapt and tweak the plan is critical. If our diary is full most of the time with tasks, emails, and meetings, it's challenging to have the energy to adapt and change to the environment that is already asking a lot from us.

One of my client's, Daniel, found the daily routine five minute check-in each morning, before touching any device or work task, to be powerful and galvanising for both his professional and personal peak performance, especially when the environment is constantly changing.

Know when you do your best thinking.

Your internal prime time is the time of day, according to your body clock, when you are the most alert and productive.

43. Forrest Gump is a 1994 American comedy-drama film directed by Robert Zemeckis and written by Eric Roth.

If you take note of how your body reacts to work at any time of day, you will be able to work out:
- when you should focus on getting work done
- when to brainstorm
- and most importantly, when you should avoid meetings or doing cognitively demanding tasks.

It is best to tackle complex projects when you are most alert. It is important to prioritise your optimum time for deep thinking throughout your day.

Brain breaks[44] and increasing oxygen are essential

The goal of brain breaks is to help your brain shift focus. Exercise increases blood flow to the brain, which helps with focus and staying alert. It also reduces stress and anxiety, making it easier to focus on crucial tasks. Research has also shown that we learn more quickly after we have exercised. We use on average 20 per cent of our oxygen and water intake to help fuel our brains.

A 5 to 15-minute brain break restores mood and elevates vigilance, and you should schedule them as you would a meeting.

- *Something beats nothing.*
  If you can take only a two-minute break, do it.

- *Moving beats stationary.*
  Get away from your desk.

- *Social beats solo.*
  A break is more restorative if you take it with somebody else (as long as you can choose with whom you spend it!).

---

44. Michael Patterson (2014) coined the term brain breaks as he came up with a design for his regular research and writing schedules. He noticed the need and devised a pattern of 17-minutes of brain work followed by intentional brain breaks of 2 to 4 minutes with a sweet spot of three minutes.

→ *Outdoors beats inside.*
　The replenishing effects of nature and fresh air are spectacular.

→ *Fully detached beats semi-detached.*
　You are better off if you don't talk about work or take your phone with you.

Along with increasing your oxygen, the result of taking a brain break is outstanding. My clients have doubled their productivity and stopped feeling totally exhausted at the end of the week.

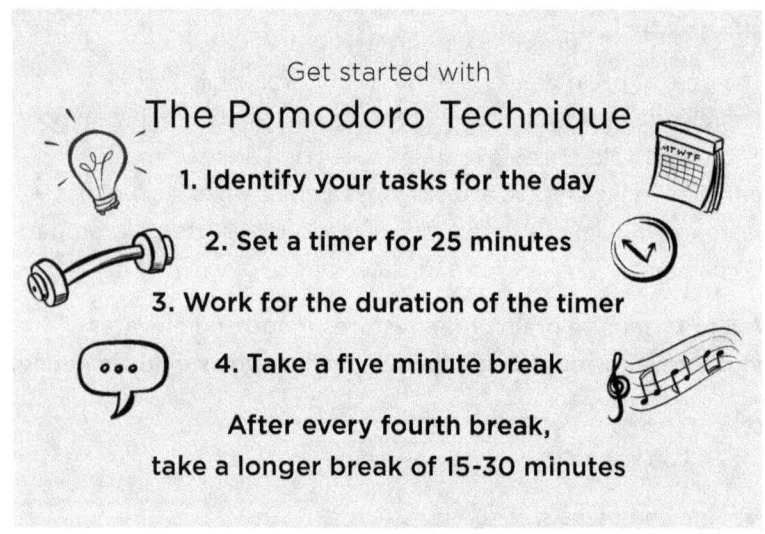

The Pomodoro technique[45] can be useful for working remotely

The technique uses a timer to break work down into intervals, traditionally 25 minutes in length, separated by short breaks.

---

45. The Pomodoro Technique is a time management method developed by Francesco Cirillo in the late 1980s. www.todoist.com/productivity-methods/pomodoro-technique   Here is a timer set up to use if required www.pomofocus.io

Protecting your time and workspace is vital

Protect your workspace

Talk to family members or roommates about the hours you are working from home and the ground rules during those hours. Assume that anything that can interrupt you, will interrupt you – such as a dog barking or someone mowing lawns in the background during a client video presentation. Be as proactive as you can about mitigating these kinds of interruptions.

Protect your time

Your time is precious and making it count is important for both professional and personal matters. Communicate with others and your manager about when you do your deep thinking, to be in your peak performance flow.

Turn off and remove things that distract you, such as messenger apps and pinging noises from notifications via your inbox or mobile phone. If anything distracts you or fights for your attention, turn it off or minimise it for specific periods of time. Communication with your key stakeholders about when you are available is vital to make this successful and sustainable.

Beware of becoming a servant to the fear of missing out (known as FOMO) or feeling it is necessary to know everything and always be contactable. Conduct a distraction audit to discover what these unnecessary distractions and fears are costing you in time and productivity, as they may be eating into your personal time for rejuvenation. Making your precious time count is important to everyone you add value to, including yourself.

Make sure you unplug - both in between and after work

Many of my clients have been struggling with unplugging from work. Here are some tips to explore:

- Set expectations regarding your availability to those you work with and those you live with. Clarify what 'urgent' may look like and the best way to communicate this effectively on both sides of the fence.
- Schedule regular blocks of time in your calendar away from your desk, for things like brain breaks.
- Have an accountability partner check in on your plan to see what is and isn't working well.
- Embrace the hobbies and interests that help you to have down time from work. I tend to work harder and faster when I know I have Zumba dance classes to look forward to and have to finish work by a particular time.
- Practise conscious self-care.

Personal and annual leave

To do our best thinking we need to have regular down time to energise our creativity and decision-making capabilities. Taking annual leave for holiday purposes has the ability to boost workplace productivity, reduce stress levels, restore our energy and improve overall mental health.

Research conducted by one of my clients, the Association of Corporate Counsel (ACC) Australia the peak body for in-house counsel (lawyers), surveyed members[46] to gain insight into the consistent and emerging challenges, working conditions and practices within in-house legal teams throughout Australia.

---

46. ACC Australia 2021 In-house counsel trends report.

In their 2021 survey, they were curious to test the hypothesis that world events in 2020 meant little uptake on personal leave. When comparing 2021 responses to that of the 2019 survey, there has been a significant drop in the number of days taken as personal / annual leave. While in 2019, almost two thirds (62%) of in-house lawyers took more than three weeks annual leave, in 2021 this dropped to just a third (36%). The number of respondents who took no leave in the past 12 months more than doubled from the previous survey, with seven percent taking no leave at all.

Executive Director, Ingrid Segota, was concerned about the added burden for in-house counsel and the increased breadth and complexity of what they were expected to achieve. As well as their normal workload, COVID-19 meant that legal departments were also managing cybersecurity concerns, staff safety and well-being while working from home, and anticipating future pandemic requirements. At the same time, significantly fewer of them were taking personal or annual leave and a harmonious work-life balance was more difficult to achieve than ever. Segota is highly aware of the importance of such balance. "Taking time off, even as micro-breaks, like a long weekend, to simply relax, refresh and recharge the mind and body has a tremendous impact on mood, health and productivity," she said.

The Australian branch of a major international not-for-profit organisation also acknowledges the importance of looking after staff and ensuring they have time to recharge personally and cater for the needs to family. It has instituted 'Well-being Wednesdays' for the foreseeable future to ensure the well-being of its staff. There is no reduction in pay. They also allow staff to work hours that help them balance the demands of home, school, family and work life while in lockdown.

My family took annual leave, sailing on a catamaran around the Whitsundays with another family for two weeks. We had limited connectivity which meant lots of activities on the water during the day like sailing, paddle boarding, snorkelling and going on walking adventures around Islands and not looking at emails, work tasks and news reports.

We replaced online activities with interpersonal activities that allowed us to appreciate our connection with one another. We were all pleasantly surprised how rejuvenated we felt on our return to Sydney, and able to deal with obstacles like COVID lock-down with a fresh approach. Our patience and understanding for one another's challenges have been remarkable since we are all working and online schooling from home. Without having this break, I am not sure we would have coped and connected as well.

Other examples of how some of my clients have set up annual and personal leave for themselves and their employees include a business owner who takes a long weekend of three to four days off every month, making sure to go somewhere different, not too far away and with limited technology devices.

People are now working longer hours and harder than ever, which has the overall effect of decreasing productivity. Some companies provide birthday leave (which employees can take as a long weekend) and doona days (complimentary time off) to reward employees with time to recover and recharge their energy. This can be a real positive for employees and boosts their sense of being valued and their overall commitment.

Practising self-care

It is imperative to take care of yourself when you work from home, which often means staying in tune with your energy levels. Telecommuters tend to take fewer sick days, often choosing to work through periods of feeling unwell.

While this may be positive for employers, and a testament to the dedication of certain telecommuters, working in relative solitude can lead you to disregard the signals from your own body. This is a slippery slope to burning out. Perhaps, more indirectly, self-care is just as vital as any other remote productivity tip.

Go outside

If you work from home, you may find yourself not leaving the house for days at a time, which is not healthy. Not only are sunlight and fresh air crucial to your health, but they will also clear your head and motivate you. Staying stuck in front of a screen all day, especially if you are tackling a difficult task, is actually detrimental to your productivity.

Get some exercise

Regular physical activity is beneficial to everyone, not just telecommuters, but they can squeeze in a workout more easily than office workers. When you need a break, don't hesitate to roll out a yoga mat, do some stretching or climb on your stationary bike for fifteen minutes. One of my clients uses a cross-trainer machine while doing online training via their TV screen, reporting being able to retain the information more effectively.

Keep mealtimes regular

Eat nutritious food and follow a meal timetable, joining with the family and or friends.

The relationship between energy and peak performance

It is impossible to maintain optimum performance without effective energy management referred to in section one 'Fuel your brain with the right ingredients'. Peak performance is defined by the state in which a person performs to the maximum of their ability.

Just do it:

Out of the list above, what could you put more attention on?

- If you did, what would this look like for your day? How would it change?
- Could this improve outcomes for you and your team?
- Could you use this list as a discussion point for your team to work out how to engage best and support each other's performance and productivity?

Remember artificial intelligence will be taking over the doing tasks, so how you set up your brain to think, innovate and make decisions effectively counts. Now is the time to learn how to harness the power of neuroscience to create more and better ways to gain perspective, rewire our brains for success, and so ensure we give the machines plenty of fruitful direction in the future. Saying you are in back-to-back meetings is essentially saying you are planning to be ineffective!

SECTION THREE

Overcoming obstacles with the brain in mind

Section Three: Overcoming obstacles with the brain in mind

Obstacles are part of life. They come in many forms, like having a large tree blocking the road when you're driving to your holiday destination, working remotely during a global pandemic, losing incorrectly saved data files, losing a big client or experiencing a health crisis. Sometimes, obstacles appear insurmountable, yet they must be overcome.

The aim of this section is to explain brain-friendly models of thinking and options allowing you to overcome obstacles without draining your precious energy and time.

The key topics covered are:

- Defining obstacles and providing common scenarios
- Why change hurts
- Emotion contagion – why emotions are not your enemy
- Resilience strategies for bouncing back from obstacles
- The art of creative problem-solving

Let's define an obstacle

The dictionary defines an obstacle as, 'something that stands in the way or that obstructs progress, a hindrance, impediment, or obstruction'.[47] Obstacles can be conceptualised as interfering forces[48] that impede the standard course of action and must be removed or otherwise dealt with if one wishes to reach the desired end-state.

Obstacles come in many shapes: physical; social; and mental. They can appear in a variety of settings (e.g., organisational, private, clinical). Potential impacts can range from signalling that an adjustment in one's thinking, or action is needed, to decelerating progress until a way to conquer the problem is found, or even bringing progress to a complete halt if it cannot be overcome.

Our perception (the eye of the beholder) of how we see things can be changed. We control how we see things and the meaning we give them. For example, when my family was in Tahiti for my 40th birthday celebrations, we were in the forest canyoning when a medium-sized spider landed on my son's helmet. I asked him to stay still, but he freaked out and threw the helmet in the river. Our tour guides explained that in Tahiti, spiders are sacred and lucky; locals don't kill or injure spiders as they believe it brings bad luck.

When I arrived back in Australia, I used this experience to change the way I perceive spiders. No longer are they horrible and scary, but rather a sign of good luck. I am proud to say I save more spiders than I kill now because I have changed my mindset. I should add, it has not changed my son's view of spiders in the slightest; his fear of spiders still outweighs their benefit.

47. Oxford English Dictionary, 2009.   48. Higgins, 2006.

Have you noticed that the more we resist life's obstacles the more stressed we feel? It seems so counterintuitive. Yet the only thing we can control in our lives is how we react to the things beyond our control. Often, we resist things that have already happened or things that may happen and this keeps us stuck, holding on to what might have been or what we wish would be.

Humans are known as time travellers, as we can go back in time through past memories and / or forward to imagined future events. Our brain is a prediction machine that craves certainty and the best way to predict the future is to create it. How we perceive and label life's experiences impacts how we store them in our brain's memory filing system. With the current overwhelm of information and because we are doing more with fewer resources and budget, we tend to primarily use our short-term memory. This means we are typically not creating enough long-term memories to draw upon for innovation and decision-making capabilities.

Recognising the mindset and lens through which you choose to view life is an important practice and having strategies that allow you to view life's daily obstacles differently present you with an opportunity.

There is a story I love in the 'letting go' series on the Breethe mediation app[49]. A young man is being chased by a tiger. He runs as fast as he can until he reaches a cliff and, having no choice, jumps off the cliff and grabs a vine over a huge waterfall. As he is dangling from the vine, he sees a growling tiger above him. The vine starts to give way, and certain death is imminent.

49. Breethe meditation and sleep app co-founded by Lynne Goldberg in 2014.

When he looks up, he notices a succulent strawberry. With no way to save his life, he decides to enjoy what he can in the moment. He reaches up, plucks the strawberry off the vine and takes a juicy bite.

Most of us fight hard against the inevitable; we fight against uncertainty, we fight against unpleasantness, we fight against change, even though we have a choice. We can choose to fight life or invite life. Things are always evolving, and our only certainty is we won't make it out of here alive. So given a choice between embracing what is, or fighting it, we can practise taking a bite of the strawberry each day. We can recognise what is and allow it to happen, investigating it with a sense of curiosity and compassion for how we feel in the moment.

I coach people around their mindset, encouraging them to:
→ Have high intention and low attachment, so there is no expectation
→ Trust in the unknown, surrender and let go
→ Understand balance and wholeness arise when we are without anxiety, to embrace non-perfection.

Aim to give your best, identify what your best looks like in terms of a plan outline (desired outcomes for you and key stakeholders, the purpose of your WHY, your unique value, next steps and timeframe), and be mindful of balancing your time and effort. This stops you over-thinking it, over-planning it and over-cooking it. Burnt toast is never palatable in my opinion!

Some of my clients express concerns about the amount of competition they face and their clients' range of choice. My response is to be memorable; tell a story that connects your audience's heart and mind. There is only one of you in the world, so STAND out and shine in the moment. Have your top three concise messages prepared. These include your purpose (that gets you out of bed), unique value and examples of how you have demonstrated it. Focus your time and energy on what you can control and influence without being attached to it.

I recall when I applied for a job and wanted it so passionately that I convinced myself I was born for the role. The head of Human Resources rang me to tell me it was a tough decision, but they had decided to give the role to another candidate with slightly more industry experience. My thinking was, you must be joking; I was born for this role, and my passion and enthusiasm is greater than any other candidate.

I cried for over a week. Little did I know the universe had bigger plans waiting for me in the IT industry.

How do I know? I ended up working in the same building and met the successful candidate from time to time. I remember thinking it was lucky I didn't get the job that I was supposedly born for.

I see now that all the connections I have in my life – work colleagues, career opportunities, existing and prospective clients – result from not getting my ideal job. I wouldn't even have met my husband or had our son if that job had taken me on a totally different path.

The key lesson I learned is to have a high intention and a low attachment to the outcome, then there is no expectation. Wanting something or someone too much can have an opposite effect to what you want. It is balancing the passion and energy into concise messages and stories of experience, and for others, it's stepping it up.

People often tell me that they don't like interviews, or don't perform well in interview settings. This is a mindset challenge, likely to be based on past experiences.

Recently a client was doing a video interview online. She was anxious about interviews and felt overwhelmed by being interviewed remotely for the first time.

To feel more confident, the client acknowledged her emotions, focused on why she was applying for the role, and then reflected on the benefits, the opportunity and the value she could contribute. We looked at the colours of her outfit to ensure the vibe matched the organisation. We practised her voice delivery, to ensure her key messages were concise, smooth, confident and memorable.

I bought my husband one of my favourite T-shirts in Tasmania. It says, "Never too young to start an empire – never too old to chase a dream". I'm a big believer that age limitations can be overcome with clearly articulating your purpose (the V and demonstrating the value you

If COVID taught us anything, it is that change is possible.
I remember seeing a quote that said, "Tradition is strong, but these times have shown us that traditions can be broken apart and reimagined."

I connect with this quote. Many of us are now approaching things with a new perspective. We may or may not be successful the first time around, but learning, unlearning and re-learning is important for our success. We will not know until we give it a go and review the learnings along the way.

As Norman Doidge, Psychiatrist put it, "Everything having to do with human training and education has to be re-examined in light of neuroplasticity".[50]

50. Dr Norman Doidge, a psychiatrist and researcher from the university of Toronto in Canada, put neuroplasticity in the spotlight in 2007 www.azquotes.com/author/18876-Norman_Doidge

Why does change hurt?

CHANGE = THREAT
→ Uncertainty
→ Effort

Providing clarity around certainty and uncertainty in a change process is especially important for success. This is often overlooked and undervalued. Some leaders assume that change always provides successful outcomes and act optimistically, but it can be costly if you don't deal with the uncertainty that change can create for your team. Some people are pessimists who find faults and fears in everything. Even so, it is important that their needs are considered in the change process.

We need people to feel certain about their purpose (the WHY behind the change and direction) and the benefits and desired outcomes (what this means for all involved) even if it's challenging. The team must understand the steps involved in moving towards the goal and be confident that potential risks will be mitigated. It is the leader's job to create a vision worth the effort required; one with sufficient certainty about where everyone will be within a timeframe.

Change can be exhausting; it can wear people out, and this is sometimes interpreted as laziness. As mentioned, our brain will run out of fuel if we don't top it up with the right ingredients throughout the day. It's like having all the apps on your mobile phone open. The device will slow down, stop working or crash, and you need to recharge or reboot it. Our brain works in a similar way.

The part of the brain known as the habit centre is the basal ganglia, located within the limbic centre (the brain's emotional centre). It is associated with various functions, including the control of voluntary motor movements, procedural learning, habit learning, eye movements, cognition and emotion. It is a prediction machine that craves certainty by creating habit short cuts, so it doesn't have to use as much energy.

Often, we try to undertake too much change too fast, and our brains go into fight, flight or freeze / threat mode. If the obstacle seems too big or there are many of them, we can't digest the change, and overwhelm and procrastination kicks in.

Tip Be curious about how you could break a goal or an obstacle into bite-sized chunks. Start with some initial probing questions to steer your thinking and planning[51].

1. Why do you want to achieve this goal and what makes it important?
2. How will you feel once you reach the goal?
3. What is the benefit of the goal?
4. Is there an expert you can call on to think through your options?
5. Are there any tools or models that could assist?
6. What are the potential obstacles (known/unknown) to achieving your goal?
7. What could motivate you when things get difficult and not go to plan?
8. What are the critical next steps and timeframe?

---

51. LinkedIn article by Robin Weninger, 2015 www.linkedin.com/pulse/setting-better-goals-10-simple-questions-stress-test-robin-weninger

What planning considerations could you propose for dealing with the unknown? I admire the work of author and neuroscientist, Dr Joe Dispenza[52]. One of his recent newsletters called Emotions are not your enemy particularly resonated with me and I would like to share parts of it with you.

....

Dr Joe Dispenza – Author, Neuroscientist

Emotions are not your enemy

Many people may have the misunderstanding that we should not feel or express emotions.

At no point when we experience a sudden loss, shock, setback, trauma and so forth have I ever suggested suppressing the corresponding emotions associated with those life events. What I have said is that the stronger the emotion we feel from some event in our outer world, the more altered we feel from our normal resting state of emotional chemical continuity in our inner world. In other words, the more powerful the emotion we experience in our internal environment, the more we pay attention to what is causing it in our external environment. As a result, this person, upset, event, encounter or experience is so powerful it captures all of our attention and as it does so, our brain takes a snapshot of that image. That snapshot is called a long-term memory, and so the memory becomes branded as a holographic image in the neural architecture of the brain.

Where problems do arise, however, is when a person gets stuck in a tumble dryer of the grieving process. What I mean by this is that instead of processing that grief, which requires them to pass through the eye of its needle by feeling the necessary

---

52. Dr. Joe Dispenza is an American neuroscientist, chiropractor, international lecturer, researcher, corporate consultant, author, and educator. Newsletter called Emotions are not your enemy Part 1, 24th August 2020.

emotions — rather than continuously circumventing or avoiding them — they just keep recycling those familiar memories and emotions throughout various experiences and interactions in their present life. If they continue living within the restricted emotional box of that past experience, then every time they experience an event that produces those same emotions to varying degrees, the trigger of those emotions places them right back in the grieving box of the past. From a biological standpoint, every time this person remembers the event, they are producing the same chemistry in their brain and body as if the event were occurring in the present moment.

Because the body is so objective — essentially, it is the unconscious mind — it believes it is in the real-life event. In this context, the body believes the event is happening over and over again. As a result, the person starts circulating the stress hormones throughout their body, when in truth they are perfectly safe in the present moment. The continuous recycling of the event, combined with the related emotions, causes the person's mind and body to become anchored in the past — in the present moment. In this context, we could say the emotion keeps terrorising them. This is the process that underpins trauma.

Learning about the brain and connecting with my body has enlightened and touched my heart and the heart of others. My insights and experiences have allowed me to help people who are experiencing tough times in practical and logical ways. My proactive approach to fuelling our brain and body, and my understanding of emotions and behaviours, helps my clients to live their best lives. I take an obstacle and turn it into an opportunity to make a difference each and every day, by supporting those around me. Every interaction I make counts, as emotions are contagious.

Emotions are contagious

Emotional contagion is the process by which an observable behavioural change in one person prompts the reflexive production of the same behaviour by others in close proximity, with the likely result of emotional convergence (Panksepp and Lahvis, 2011[53]).

Regulating emotions contributes to how we bounce back from obstacles, hardship, disappointments, uncertainty and unexpected change. How you show up every day and respond to life and work challenges affects those around you. You can affect the performance and productivity of those around you if you're in a bad mood or sending out negative energy. The reverse is also true; if you are happy, joyous, positive and calm, you can lift the performance and productivity of those around you.

In our current frenetic world, being calm is critical to creating ideas and solutions, and making sound decisions. I don't recommend making important decisions when your emotions are heightened, as it can cause more challenges than you bargained for.

Emotions are like the weather – you get to decide each day whether you are bringing the sunshine, clouds, rain or lightening.

Lynne Goldberg[54], co-founder of the Breethe meditation and mindfulness app, has a technique for regulating emotion and building resilience. It is called. **R.A.I.N**:

Recognise

Allow

Investigate

Non-identify – which means letting go of the attachment.

---

53. ScienceDirect article, 2016 www.sciencedirect.com/topics/psychology/emotional-contagion
54. Breethe meditation app, 2014 - designed as an inner wellness partner for anxiety, stress, sleep, and more. www.breethe.com

There are three obstacles that prevent us from showing up positively and calmly, for ourselves and others. They are most common when we are under threat.

FIGHT

1. **FIGHT** - We go out in the rain and forget an umbrella, so we tell ourselves we are such an idiot; 'I'm so dumb for forgetting to pack an umbrella.'

2. **FLIGHT** - We flee or avoid. We avoid unpleasant conversations, people or situations.

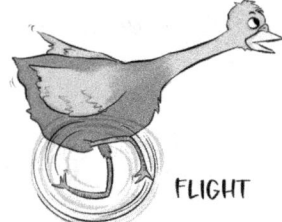

FLIGHT

3. **FREEZE** - We freeze, or don't do anything, hoping not to be noticed. We may know the situation is bad but like a proverbial ostrich who puts its head in the sand, we pretend it's not happening.

FREEZE

In all of these situations, we create some form of resistance to what is. We are not bringing the awareness, acceptance, curiosity and the letting go of the R.A.I.N technique to the experience. Let's look at the R.A.I.N four step practice:

Recognise

We first bring awareness to the emotion by bringing our PFC online to analyse the limbic centre.

Allow

We do not resist in any way, just observe it. We allow our mind to be the sky and the emotions to be the clouds.

Investigate

We look at our reactions with curiosity, perhaps asking, "What has been the trigger?" or "How has this made me feel?"

Non-identify

We let it go without making it personal to us (breathing deeply helps) or we reframe it by seeing how it can be viewed from a different lens or perspective. You can choose to channel someone else's thinking. Try asking, "How would Bill Gates, co-founder of Microsoft or Richard Branson, founder of Virgin, view this situation?" Or identify what options they would consider.

Just do it:

Be curious about options that can help you change gears. Positive activities like exercise, music, dancing, gardening or playing with your pet can lift your spirits. Identify your 'go-to' options that work in different threat scenarios. Prioritise your three strategies and focus on these for the next two weeks, then evaluate what is and isn't working for you. You may have to tweak them before creating a habit.

This technique is giving your mind complete freedom to see obstacles and behaviours in new ways, without attaching ourselves to the emotional reaction.

Resilience strategies for overcoming obstacles

When I worked for an IT security organisation, the company offered clients a fantastic service called an Incident Response Plan. This was a set of instructions to help clients mitigate any potential IT security risks and breaches, and so reduce the chances of cybercrime, data loss and service outages that threaten daily work.

We sometimes have great processes like this in place for our professional lives, but not when dealing with our day-to-day challenges. We don't have a resilience plan in place, as we do for a fire drill.

A resilience plan approach for work situations

This is for when things don't go to plan, or you're dealing with the unknown. I recommend answering these questions while in a calm state before an incident, obstacle or threat state occurs.

Introducing the P.I.R Model to prime the brain for obstacles

1. **Proactive protection** – What can you do every day to prevent known and unknown issues from interfering with your plan, goal or intention? Examples: Exercising, taking brain breaks, protecting your deep-thinking time, prioritising tasks, scheduling time in your diary for the unknown and reflecting on what is and isn't working.

   Identify your threat and reward triggers (from 'How the brain works' section). What is in your circle of influence? What do you spend significant time thinking about, even though you have no control nor influence over the outcome? What can you do to mitigate or reduce the risk?

2. **Incident response** – Consider the steps, processes, and options at your disposal. Identify people who can provide advice depending on the obstacle or incident. Consider creating a communication plan that incorporates internal and external stakeholders. Check that your 'go-to' people are happy to be on call and know how best to reach them.

Tip Have some draft communications prepared ahead of time, so all you need to do is fill in the detail / blanks of your particular challenge.

What are some of the goal posts you can move closer? Feeling like you have accomplished even a small task will keep you motivated. Feeling 'on purpose' in your work is a key contributor to positive emotional wellbeing.

3. **Remediation** – What is your plan for applying the key learnings and removing the issue, challenge or obstacle for the next time you face a similar challenge? Aim not only to quarantine the problem but prevent it reoccurring. It's time to get off the roundabout of doing the same thing repeatedly and expecting a different outcome (the definition of insanity).

The art to creative problem-solving

When it comes to generating ideas, identifying options, or finding solutions to problems, our brain is like a filing cabinet system. We tend to use the first drawer in the cabinet (our short-term memory) for our initial ideas, especially if we feel under pressure to deliver. For some people, the first idea may be the best option.

In this section we will be exploring a model called the polarity management tool that I have found particularly useful for my clients to help with critical and creative thinking.

Polarity management tool

Polarity thinking, a term coined by Barry Johnson[55], describes situations where there are truth and wisdom on more than one side of an issue; each side is incomplete without the other's wisdom and input. There are two sides of a coin.

The polarity management exercise will help you distinguish

---

55. Barry Johnson, 1998 The Polarity Management™ model and created a set of principles to deal with all polarities in life. This tool was provided during the Advance Diploma of Neuroscience of leadership at Neurocapability, 2017.

between solvable problems and polarities and help you effectively manage those polarities most important to you and your organisation's success.

I came across this tool when studying neuroscience of leadership and have used it with clients to weigh up choices and decisions; between jobs and companies, candidates for a job role, making major purchases like property, property locations, investments, cars, and strategic business decisions. It provides a deeper level of clarity. It helps to broaden thinking by moving away from black and white thinking.

What is good about the current situation? (1)	**What advantages might the change result in? (4)**
What is not working in the current situation? (3)	**What are your concerns about what the change might result in? (2)**

 Just do it:

Identify in one sentence an obstacle / problem you want to solve. Divide a sheet of paper or word document into four quadrants to mirror the above.

Step 1: Write down all your ideas about what is good about the current situation in the top left quadrant. These are current advantages. List options until you have exhausted all possibilities (just like the divergent thinking model mentioned above). If you are doing this with a group, make sure you get everyone's ideas until they have run out of suggestions.

Step 2: Move to the bottom right quadrant and list the future disadvantages. Identify all the concerns about what may happen if the change or potential solution was implemented. Do this until you have exhausted all possibilities.

Step 3: Move to the lower left quadrant and identify what is not working in the current situation. Keep working until you have exhausted all possibilities.

Step 4: In the upper right quadrant, list future advantages, benefits and outcomes that could result from the change or solving the problem.

Reflection questions:

→ Reflect for a moment on what you have come up with

→ Did you have key insights[56] or AHA moments that changed your thinking?

→ How can you retain the benefits of what is working now and take them into the future situation without feeling daunted? Often the solution is tweaking the current process, without having to throw the baby out with the bath water. We often need to examine how we view a situation and how else we could view it by pausing and reflecting on our thinking

→ How can you guard against future disadvantages or minimise the negative impact? This is useful for broadening your thinking and priming your brain against potential obstacles.

Recently I used this polarity management exercise on a coaching client whose obstacle was selecting between two job roles. It was a highly effective exercise for identifying

---

56. Insight definition: The sudden reorganisation of knowledge resulting in a new understanding or solution to a problem. Insight processes that peak in 'unpredictable moments of exceptional thinking' are often referred to as 'AHA' or 'Eureka' moments.

the obstacles (red flags) for each of the two job roles and companies. This allowed my client to have an open conversation with the hiring managers and make an informed decision.

Obstacles come in all shapes and sizes that every human being must deal with regardless of who and where you come from. How you perceive and approach the obstacle is key to the choices you make and the outcomes of your decisions. In my experience it is not what happens to you, more importantly how you respond.

SECTION FOUR

....

Drive the right behaviours, mindset and passion for achieving your desired outcomes

....

Section Four:

Drive the right behaviours, mindset and passion for achieving your desired outcomes.

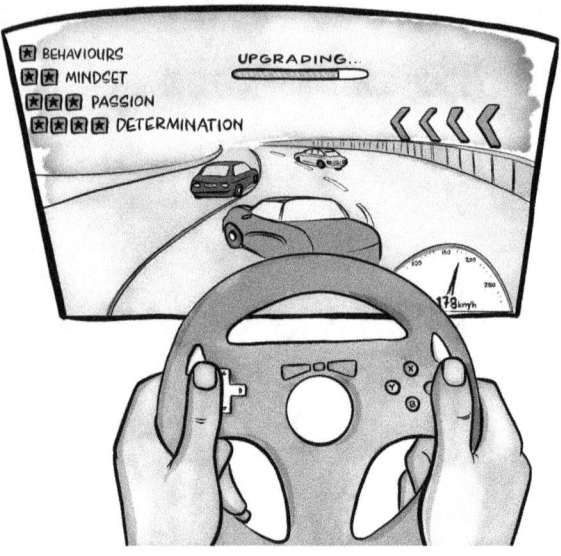

Reflect on the last time you created a new behaviour to achieve a specific intention or outcome. How much time and energy did it take? What were the key drivers for making a change in the first place?

We tend to change when we experience significant pain (threat) or pleasure (reward). A key element to successful behavioural change is minimising perceived threats and maximising the positive feelings generated through the brain's reward circuitry.

Many of our daily actions are automatic, as your brain is on autopilot 95 per cent of the time[57]. This is how it conserves energy. For better or worse, ultimately our habits shape us and breaking a bad habit is about rewiring your brain.

57. Daniel Kahneman, a Senior scholar at Princeton University, author of Thinking, fast and slow, 2011.

The more often you perform an action or behave a certain way, the more it gets physically 'wired' into your brain. Our brain changes its shape in response to behaviours and thoughts we repeat, which create new connections. These new connections can be thought of as new 'wiring' that allows new behaviours and thoughts to become entrenched. This amazing adaptive quality of your brain is known as neuroplasticity, the ability to reorganise itself by forming new connections between brain cells (neurons). Learning new things is important to our health and well-being, as it helps our brains form new neural connections.

As mentioned, our brain forms neuronal connections based on what you repeatedly do — both good and bad. Every time you act in the same way, a specific neuronal pattern is stimulated and becomes strengthened in your brain.

Habits are the brain's internal drivers. If you want to change, you need to create a sustainable plan to create new wiring. This requires breaking it down into brain friendly chunks, tapping into the reward circuitry and releasing dopamine along the way.

Dopamine is a neurotransmitter and like all neurotransmitters is a chemical that the brain uses to signal specific neurons under specific conditions. It controls not only mental and emotional responses, but also motor reactions. Dopamine is known as the 'pleasure hormone' and plays a significant role in driving behaviour. It is responsible for us experiencing happiness and joy; I call it the natural 'feel good drug'. It is important to choose behaviours that support the release of as much dopamine as you can when 'wiring' a new habit, as you are more likely to pursue the new habit / routine and stick to it. A routine repeated becomes a habit.

When you first adopt a new behaviour, you have to engage our PFC, the thinking rational brain, and insert conscious effort, intention and thought into the process. When you have performed the new routine enough times for connections to be made and strengthened in your brain, the behaviour will require less effort as it becomes the new habit.

The brain needs a lot of energy to function optimally and protects its energy reserves as it is our primary survival organ. One way in which it protects its reserves is to push back against any changes we try to make. Many of us lack enough energy and the right-thinking habits to make behavioural changes to reach our goals and intentions.

Key ingredients required for behavioural change are passion, determination, consistency, repetition, energy, time, focus, reward state, reflection, positive mindset and feedback / support. Change also requires a thinking model that will allow you to drive the right behaviours to achieve your desired outcomes.

I created the D.R.I.V.E. model to help my clients with their thinking, planning and decision-making capability when committing to behavioural change. The D.R.I.V.E. model stands for:

D**etermine your purpose and passion** – gain clarity about your vision for success; what does it look like, feel like and taste like?

R**eflect on your thinking** – consider the behaviours and mindset you need to reach your vision

I** am statements for self-affirmation** – engage the brain circuits connected with self-processing and reward

V**ulnerability** – identify the blockages that hold you back and reappraise thinking to change your perception: perception is your reality

E**xert energy to learn something new** – determine the area where you would like to improve your knowledge and skills: we are learning beings, and the lifelong process of learning, regardless of age, is what makes us human and allows us to evolve.

Determine your purpose

Gain clarity on your vision and passion for success – what does it look like, feel like and taste like?

It is important to clarify your sense of purpose and what you are truly passionate about. This helps you find and do things that add meaning to your life, and cope when things don't go to plan. It increases your grit and determination. A healthy sense of purpose helps you put negative events in perspective, to refocus on the things that are meaningful to you and move ahead and enjoy life when obstacles arise.

Clearly articulating your purpose helps you differentiate between the important and unimportant, and aids the decision-making process. But functioning at today's fast pace impacts the way we live our lives, how we code short and long-term memories and our physical and mental health.

As a personality trait[58], grit is one type that involves striving to achieve long-term goals with continual passion and perseverance. It plays an extremely crucial role in personal achievement.

Broadly, grit is a subcomponent of the complex construct of self-regulation and mounting empirical evidence indicates that the PFC is closely associated with self-regulation. The findings suggest that the PFC, which is related to goal-directed thought and behaviour, task management and planning, and cognitive control, may play an essential role in personality differences in grit.

My son, Caleb, whose passion is rock climbing, had a goal to climb a particularly difficult level climb before 16 years of age. He had this goal for several months and came close to

---

58. American psychological association dictionary definition of a personality trait relatively stable, consistent, and enduring internal characteristic that is inferred from a pattern of behaviors, attitudes, feelings, and habits in the individual.

achieving it on several occasions, and it was frustrating for him to get so close and not accomplish it. On the last night before his birthday, he was determined and hungry to achieve this goal. My husband, Jon, said Caleb was pumped and had a determination in his eye's that Jon had not seen in his previous attempts; it was pure grit and determination. Caleb told himself he was going to hang on, no matter what. His eyes were filled with pure glee and delight as he slammed himself onto the last hold at the top. Caleb experienced every sensation of the reward circuitry as he ran around the climbing gym, feeling the full force of the dopamine rush through his brain and body. When he walked through the front door that evening like a champion, his smile of achievement was priceless.

The next time Caleb faces a challenge or obstacle in his life and needs to bounce back (resilience building), I will use this example of grit and determination to help him to tap into the reward circuitry of accomplishment, even when it's tough and tiring.

One of my favourite models for defining purpose is by Simon Sinek[59]; START WITH WHY. Sinek believes in a bright future and our ability to build it together. He discovered remarkable patterns in how the greatest leaders and organisations think, act and communicate. He may be known for popularising the concept of START WITH WHY in his first TED Talk in 2009 and then with his book. I recommend viewing the five-minute TED Talk – the link is in the reference section.

THE GOLDEN CIRCLE

WHY?
HOW?
WHAT?

Diagram source: Simon Sinek

[59]. Simon Sinek is a British-American author and inspirational speaker. He is the author of five books, including START WITH WHY, 2009.

What is your WHY / purpose? What is a great goal in this area? How important is it to you to achieve this (on a scale of one to ten)?

It took me many attempts to get my WHY right. I am sharing it with you as I know a number of people struggle to articulate their WHY and providing my example may assist your thinking.

My 'WHY' improves the lives, productivity and performance of individuals, teams and organisations while impacting their health and well-being positively. I harness neuroscience research to provide brain friendly education to successfully manage a forever changing landscape.

Adapting is key to our survival, along with living a healthy balanced lifestyle.

My 'WHY' is tied to my core values of:

- Making a difference
- Curiosity
- Gratitude
- Health and well-being
- Learning and growth.

Tips if you are stuck on defining your purpose or goal

- If you are unsure about your goal / purpose, I suggest listing your core values (top three to five) and why it is important to you in your work and or life. Identify what you are most passionate about.

- Once you have your passion list, compare it against your top values, then rank the importance of each one on a scale of one to ten (ten being most important).

This will help you distil what is most important to you.

The key to achieving goals is visualising the internal and external environment that creates the result you aim for and maximises what energises you naturally.

Top performers and successful professionals and leaders have a clearly defined purpose, meaning, mastery (based on working on the skills required over a period) and their passion drives enthusiasm and motivation.

Reflect on your thinking, and the behaviours you need to reach your vision

How often do you reflect on your thinking and behaviours to reach your purpose?

Often, we are so busy that we don't prioritise time to reflect on our thinking and behaviours required to achieve our WHY / purpose. Over time, some of the behaviours that have helped you be successful may no longer serve your purpose. Your purpose may have changed direction as you've grown and developed over the years.

Regularly dedicating reflective time to creating a compelling vision of the life you want is one of the most effective strategies for achieving the life of your dreams. Perhaps the best way to look at the concept of a life vision is as a compass to help guide you to take the best actions and make the right decisions to propel you toward your best life.

Why you need a vision

One of my favourite quotes, adapted from Lewis Carroll's Alice in Wonderland is, 'If you don't know where you are going, how will you know when you get there?' With a vision in mind, you are more likely to succeed far beyond what you will achieve without a clear vision. Think of crafting your life vision as mapping a path to your personal and professional dreams. Life satisfaction and personal happiness are within reach. If you do not develop your vision, other people, the environment, and circumstances will direct the course of your life.

Clients have asked for my help as they no longer want to just go with the flow; they want to create a path that adds the most value and contribution. Here are the steps I recommend, and it starts with creating a vision board.

What is a vision board?

Your vision board is a unique visualisation tool that creates a space to define your goals. Think of it as a map of your future that will inspire and help create a vibrational match for the future you desire daily. Use this to create your desired career, relationship, income level, or anything important to you.

Steps to create your vision board:

1. Complete the previous steps of defining your purpose and goals, along with your top three to five values

2. Identify the actions you need to take to achieve your vision goals. Use photographs, images from the web - whatever inspires you.

3. Make a collage of all these images on a bulletin board, wall, A4 paper that you can laminate or put in a binder. Feel free to get creative! Consider including a picture of yourself in a happy reward state – what would this look like? Feel like?

4. Tip: avoid creating a cluttered or chaotic board – to avoid attracting chaos into your life. Simplicity is the best.

5. Add motivational 'affirmation words' and inspiring quotes that represent how you want to FEEL. Choose words like 'courage,' 'brave,' 'free,' 'creative freedom,' 'belonging,' or 'orchestrator.' Take a few moments to review your vision board every day, especially when you wake up and before you go to bed. You can use it while doing yoga or meditation, intention setting or look at it when you are relaxing.

I am statements for self-affirmation

Self-affirmation engages brain circuits connected with self-processing and reward. When self-competence is endangered, self-affirmations can help restore it by allowing people to reflect on sources of self-worth, such as essential values.

An fMRI study was conducted comparing participants who used self-affirmation vs those who did not. Results showed that there was an increased activity in the brain self-processing system (medial prefrontal cortex and posterior cingulate cortex) and valuation system (ventral striatum and ventral medial prefrontal cortex) when participants focused and reflected upon future-oriented core values.[60]

What is an 'I am' statement?

The 'I am' statement uses self-affirmation to instruct our brain to create reality. It is any sentence that begins with the words 'I am'.

What makes 'I am' statements so powerful?

Speaking those two words of 'I am', along with conscious intent, connects us to our positive energy source within a reward state. The opposite takes our energy and power away when we say things like I am useless, hopeless, no good and stupid.

When we use self-affirmation such as, 'I am this' or 'I am that' this gives specific and direct instruction about how we perceive ourselves. Perception becomes our reality the more it is repeated and reflected upon.

Examples of some of my own 'I am' statements that have helped me reach my vision board mentioned previously are:

➔ I am gifted with helping people to overcome their obstacles. This is my contribution and purpose in making a difference in the lives of others and is a big part of WHY I do what I do.

➔ I am free to be my best self, even though I make mistakes. Mistakes are a gift because they help me to learn, grow, change and adapt.

➔ I am an author of greatness, as I have many experiences to share from myself and those of my clients that will add value in the lives of others.

60. Oxford Academic, Social Cognitive and Affective Neuroscience Journal, Matthew D. Lieberman et al., (2015). www.academic.oup.com/scan/article/11/4/621/2375054?login=true

Examples of my clients that empowered their vision

→ I am the orchestrator of my life, and I empower myself to lead from my authentic self-belief.

→ I am free to construct, create, innovate and help my clients be successful.

→ I am grateful for my capability to learn new things that give me future opportunities.

How do you make an 'I am' statement?

The way to make a powerful 'I am' statement is to be clear about the reality you want to create. Imagine yourself there now, and then describe it beginning with the words, 'I am.'

It is best when you use your everyday language. The more it sounds like you, the more credible the instruction feels.

Once the 'I am' statement is created, it works best when using it on a regular basis. You need to speak it daily and repeat it until it becomes your truth and, a part of your subconscious habit centre (basil ganglia).

While it's fine to write down or recite positive affirmations in your thoughts, it will take a long time for connections to form in your memory pathway within the limbic system. While these are powerful in and of themselves, repeating them aloud elicits a powerful emotion and energy that reinforces the words in both your mind and body.

 **Just do it:**

I recommend consider using your 'I am' statements as an extension of your vision board and have them in places you can view them regularly and easily i.e bathroom mirror, screen saver, fridge, next to your bed and desk.

Vulnerability

It is time to identify the blockages that hold you back and reappraise your thinking so you can change your perception. Perception is your reality; reevaluate it and you may gain a different perspective.

A quote from Joseph Campbell[61] that is dear to my heart is, "The cave you fear to enter holds the treasure you seek."

This quote resonated deeply for me when I was writing this book. I procrastinated and made every excuse under the sun for why I couldn't start. I needed to focus on generating business to pay for the book, my family commitments were important, as was keeping fit and healthy – the excuses never stopped. Encouragement from my family, friends, book coach, editor, and clients didn't move the needle. Even when I allocated writing time in my diary, having a planned content approach normally works for me – I was stuck.

What was the tipping point?

Facing my fears, some of which were hidden in my subconscious. I didn't know what was holding me back until I read Dare to Lead, by Brene Brown[62], an expert in the power of vulnerability. Brene Brown is authentic and humorous in her approach to her specialty and I love her work.

Brene Brown shared an example of a metaphorical cave she feared entering; she admitted that she didn't know how to do some of the things that she thought 'real leaders' can do. One of these areas was project time-management. Her lack of confidence left her feeling stuck, scared, tired and lonely at times.

---

61. Joseph Campbell was renowned for teaching about the mythologies of many cultures. 62. Brené Brown is an American professor, lecturer, author, netflix documentary and podcast host. Brown has spent decades studying the topics of courage, vulnerability, shame, and empathy.

Brene Brown's team were frustrated by her unrealistic deadlines and when they responded, Brown's fear behaviours kicked-in and caused a bottleneck in productivity. By brainstorming ideas on how to deal with this dynamic, the team uncovered ways to move forward and achieve an amazing outcome for everyone.

I was curious about the loneliness Brene Brown spoke about, and this reflection led to my 'AHA' moment. The cave I feared entering was the isolation and loneliness of writing the book on my own. I love presenting in front of an audience, engaging with people. I do my best work when I'm sharing, listening, connecting, collaborating and engaging with others for the greater good.

COVID had impacted my business, and some of my speaking events and training workshops were cancelled. Even though I adapted by promoting my services online, learning new technologies and spending the time I saved on travel with my family or exercising with my girlfriends, I couldn't find the time to write the book I'd dreamed about for years.

COVID has shown me how much I missed working face-to-face with like-minded people and being challenged by their obstacles. I work better when I have lots of client projects on. When they taper off, and I face multiple administrative tasks that are not directly people-oriented, my motivation dips and I procrastinate.

I realised that my real fear was that I saw writing as a lonely process. Acknowledging that fear took a huge weight off my shoulders.

Additionally, this primary fear opened up other insecurities that had hung around from my school days, when I struggled with reading and writing despite my grit and determination. In my subconscious, the self-doubt chatter asked if I was good enough, unique enough and could add the value, power, wisdom to serve others the way I have always wanted to. My underlying fear was not wanting to be ordinary; life is too short not to make a significant difference.

Once I understood my reluctance to tackle the book, I reevaluated how I could view this obstacle as an opportunity. When I encounter a challenge like this, the thinking I go through is: when I am on my death bed, and I look back on my life, what do I want to see? I need to know that I gave something my best shot at being extraordinary. I don't want to die wondering what could have been. I see learning as the key to life, and I knew my life would be richer by overcoming my fear of writing. I realised that being an author would be a life-changing experience, one I could share with the people I collaborate with, to bring this knowledge to you.

Tips for dealing with vulnerability:

→ Be curious about what is holding you back, increase your oxygen levels to create mental capacity and or use mindfulness practices mentioned in section 1, 'Fuel your brain'

→ Reappraise how you view this fear or obstacle. Who do you know who has had a similar experience and may be able to provide insights? Where do you do your best thinking and when are you in a relaxed state?

→ Learn something new, pick up a book, download an audio-book, do a course, watch a TED talk or podcast. Exposure to new ideas, fresh modes of thinking, and diverse knowledge creates new neural connections. These will stimulate your brain to devise new and different solutions. Knowledge is powerful. Reading Brene Brown's book helped give me insights into a fear I couldn't articulate until I related it to someone else's experience (neuroscience calls this mirroring – seeing ourselves in someone else's experiences).

Initially fear may still be in the back of your mind but focusing on the opportunity, desired outcomes and what you may gain will outweigh the fears and, over time, this will become your new habit.

Fear of the unknown is perhaps the fundamental fear that underlies all of our very human anxieties and worries.

"The oldest and strongest emotion of mankind is fear, and the oldest and strongest kind of fear is fear of the unknown" by Dr Sarah McKay[63] – PhD Neuroscientist.

What impact does FEAR have on your productivity?

The story of my writer's block shows how vulnerability and fear go together. Unless we understand the fear underlying our sense of vulnerability, it is hard to be courageous.

Fear is the biggest goal and productivity killer. It is a human emotion that is triggered by a perceived threat.

A basic survival mechanism alerts our bodies to respond to danger with a fight, flight or freeze response. Our brain is geared more for a threat than a reward state. When we experience our threat response, it takes longer to recover and impacts our ability to think and make decisions clearly.

How are you currently controlling your fear, uncertainty, and doubts (F.U.Ds) so they don't impact your opportunities and important decisions?

63. Dr Sarah McKay, Neuroscientist, quote from LinkedIn article 'Fear of the unknown. 7 strategies to build a resilient brain in uncertain times' – April 2020.

Our thoughts can be impacted by the impostor syndrome, the persistent inability to believe that one's success is deserved or has been legitimately achieved as a result of one's own efforts or skills (self-doubt related to work accomplishments)' whispering words of uncertainty. It starts as a niggle like: 'Oh, you cannot achieve that goal; the target is way too high; this organisation is dreaming.'

The Asana Anatomy of Work Index 2021, showed 68% of Australian and New Zealand workers and 74% of Singapore workers have experienced imposter syndrome over the past year, which is higher than the global average of 62%[64].

Strategies to control the impostor syndrome

Be aware – We need to cultivate conscious awareness as we are on autopilot 95 per cent of the time. Realise that this monster will attack the vulnerable. Identify your personal F.U.Ds (threat triggers, i.e. when you make a mistake)?

Catch it early – If you feel the first niggle, take stock. Understand the situation and realise that the monster is trying to feed. Breathe deeply, release it by letting go or replace it with a positive thought, i.e. instead of calling yourself an idiot when you make a mistake, you can reframe it by asking self, "What can I learn from this experience? What is the opportunity to grow?" Getting the brain curious is gold, as you are triggering a reward state.

Identify the value you contribute - List the value you contribute and how you make a difference in terms of outcomes. No two brains are the same, so you will bring a unique perspective.

Celebrate the wins - Realise your self-worth, celebrate, and reward yourself for overcoming a hurdle or thinking differently.

64. Asana Anatomy of Work Index 2021. Accessed from: www.asana.com/resources/anatomy-of-work In October 2020, quantitative research was conducted by Sapio Research on behalf of Asana, to understand how people spend time at work.

What rewards / outcomes would incentivise you to think differently?

Kill the impostor - Most successful people rewire their beliefs and values about themselves. They can do it; you can too! The 'I am' statements for self-affirmation can replace the impostor.

Exert energy to learn something new

We are learning beings, and the lifelong process of learning, regardless of age, is what makes us human and makes our lives worthwhile. Let's consider some of the following advantages:

→ Having a diverse set of skills allows us to bring a variety of viewpoints to our discussions

→ Learning allows us to adjust to new conditions more quickly and effortlessly

→ Having a comprehensive understanding of unknown situations fosters innovation by encouraging us to think creatively and solve problems in novel ways

→ Learning strengthens our character and makes us more motivating to people around us.

What does it mean to say we have learned something?

There is a physical change in our brain when we learn something new, according to research (The New Science of Learning, by Terry Doyle and Todd Zakrajsek, 2018). Our brain contains about 86 billion neurons, each of which may create up to 10,000 connections with other neurons, allowing the brain to adapt to new information on a continuous basis. These new networks have the ability to generate long-term memories if they are activated and trained regularly. The connections between brain cells become stronger every time you exercise newly learned information or skills, and your capacity to recall the material becomes easier and faster as well.

Ideas for learning something new

In order to gain a new perspective and learn something new, the following are some ideas to consider against your purpose, passion, vision and future career opportunities:

- Gain a new or additional qualification, certificate, or short course
- Learn a new language
- Listen to podcasts
- Watch TED talks and documentaries that inspire new thinking and ideas
- Subscribe to a book club or gain new knowledge from reading
- Search out new activities or games to play.

Expanding on some of the ideas listed, my family has been exploring new activities recently. These include sailing, snorkelling in different locations, card games, listening to audio books before going to sleep and learning new ball games like ping pong. This has allowed all of us to learn something new, enhance our connection with one another, reduce stress, gain new insights[65] known as 'aha' moments and have fun at the same time increasing our energy levels.

Learning a new language helps connect information from both hemispheres of the brain. One of the learning habit activities

---

65. Insight definition: The sudden reorganisation of knowledge resulting in a new understanding or solution to a problem. Insight processes that peak in 'unpredictable moments of exceptional thinking' are often referred to as 'AHA' or 'Eureka' moments.

I do with clients to demonstrate neuroplasticity in action (the brain's ability to create new wiring) is to learn a new greeting in another language over a two week period. As an example, saying good morning in Japanese, 'ohayo-gozaimasu' and good morning everyone 'minasan ohayo-gozaimasu'. The results include creating curiosity and connection with their colleagues, manager and employees by exerting a new energy when starting the day (a great conversation starter).

A documentary that inspired new learnings on achieving our family vision was My Octopus Teacher. The Netflix original documentary film was directed by Pippa Ehrlich and James Reed and starred Craig Foster, who also produced the film.

Craig Foster found his way back from a debilitating disenchantment with life to discover a renewed sense of purpose through reconnecting with nature. The film's location at the juncture of untamed land and sea at the very tip of South Africa is just astounding, and the relationship Craig Foster develops with the intensely beautiful and intelligent female octopus is utterly mesmerizing.

The film imparts a critical lesson about nature's healing power and the human necessity to interact with nature and be spectators. It is a brilliant documentary to review when reflecting on social isolation and the challenges of COVID. My Octopus Teacher may just convince you that our salvation from loneliness may lie in making deep and nurturing connections with the astonishing natural world around us.

Craig Foster's story ties in well with the passion that my husband and I have for the sea. We have a vision to sail around the world and connect to and experience nature. We intend to take our followers along by filming our experiences and learnings, to show people how to create a purpose-path and fulfil it in brain friendly ways. Stay tuned for more about this in the next few years.

We are social beings born to connect with each other. In my view, we need to take stock of what's important to us and how we want to contribute to this amazing planet and ensure we make our precious energy and time count.

Another inspirational story that exerted new energy within me is Terri Irwin a naturalist, animal conservationist and the owner of Queensland's Australia Zoo. Terri's story is one of animal conservation and her love for, and tragic loss of her husband, Steve Irwin. Terri Irwin is carrying on the couple's vision to make the world a better place through nature and animal conservation efforts and caring for her children.

In an interview on free-to-air TV, Terri Irwin recalled some of her key obstacles, including losing Steve, and finding a way to fulfil their higher purpose and vision for nature and animal conservation. It is her family's legacy and the difference she wants to make to the planet.

Listening to her story, I put myself in her shoes, and I had a powerful 'insight – aha learning moment' for myself. I could see parts of myself in Terri's story because I realised that I am in the business of human conservation. Why? To help people to overcome the stresses, obstacles, overwhelming pressures of everyday life.

Individuals are burning out with huge to-do lists, overwhelmed by urgent deadlines that eat away at critical thinking, imagination, judgement, and mental and physical health. This is why exerting your energy by learning something new is a powerful way to grow and reach your goals.

Just do it:

1. Write down a list of learning options where you could exert your energy.
2. Prioritise your top three and explain why you selected these.
3. Identify how they are linked to your purpose, passion, vision board and 'I am' statements.

This brings us to the end of section 4 – 'Drive the right behaviours, mindset and passion for achieving your desired outcomes'. In summary the D.R.I.V.E model is created to help improve your thinking, planning and decision-making capability when committing to behavioural change. D.R.I.V.E stands for:

Determine your purpose and passion – gain clarity about your vision for success; what does it look like, feel like and taste like?

Reflect on your thinking – consider the behaviours and mindset you need to reach your vision

I am statements for self-affirmation – engage the brain circuits connected with self-processing and reward

Vulnerability – identify the blockages that hold you back and reappraise thinking to change your perception: perception is your reality

Exert energy to learn something new – determine the area where you would like to improve your knowledge and skills: we are learning beings, and the lifelong process of learning, regardless of age, is what makes us human and allows us to evolve.

I recommend initially selecting one area of focus from the D.R.I.V.E model over a 90 day period. In my experience, it takes approximately 90 days to create a new behavioural habit. Consider the milestones by breaking it down into small digestible steps along the 90 days and how you plan to celebrate the wins along the way and whom you can share it with. Think about the rewards, benefits and outcomes this would give you and the impact on those around you.

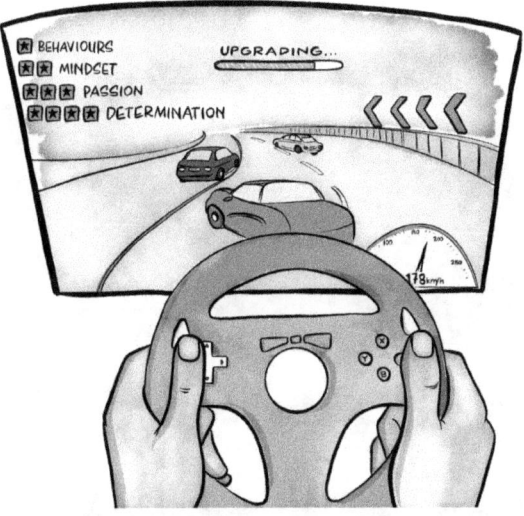

Conclusion

Conclusion

Reap what you sow to create the life you deserve

The brain is like a garden: you can sow a seed and it can grow into a strong, healthy tree if the conditions are set up for success.

The seed that is sown can represent empathy and goodness or you can let the weeds of doubt, pressure and life's challenges overrun your garden. A threat state can take over and control your emotions and your outcome. But it is up to you which seeds you plant, the focus you choose to give them and the path you forge ahead on, regardless of the obstacles and environmental changes you encounter along the way.

Professional and personal success is not just about planting the seed; success depends on the quality of the soil and establishing the right environmental conditions to grow in your chosen direction. The elements will test your garden; your environment will change, but every storm, drought or disaster

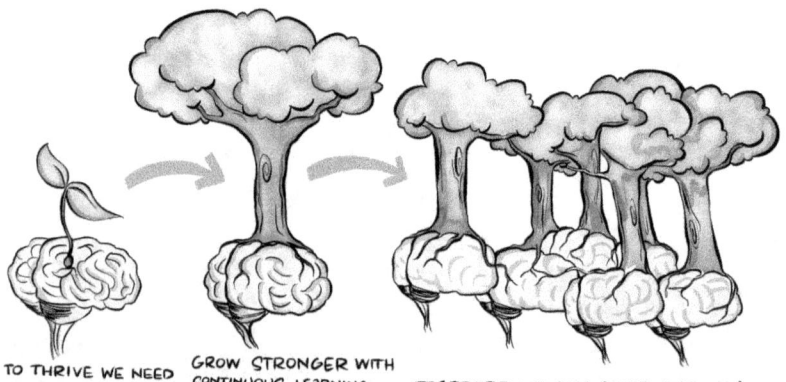

TO THRIVE WE NEED QUALITY SOIL & THE RIGHT ENVIRONMENT

GROW STRONGER WITH CONTINUOUS LEARNING, INSIGHTS & IMPROVEMENT ALONG the WAY

TOGETHER WE CAN ACHIEVE MORE!

is an opportunity to learn, adapt, grow and become your best self and make a difference in the lives of those around you.

Obstacles and disasters can bring people together and cultivate new and stronger connections that are valuable.

It is my aim to help your brain minimise or get rid of the weeds that weigh you down and to give you the right recipe to '*Rewire for Success*' with the F.O.O.D framework:

Fuelling your brain with the right ingredients

Organising your daily structure based on where and when you do your best thinking

Overcoming obstacles with the brain in mind

Driving the right behaviours, mindset and passion to achieve your desired outcomes.

The F.O.O.D framework is designed to be digested one bite at a time and it's up to you where your start.

Identify 1-3 areas that are your top priorities right now and go through the following:

- **REVIEW** – your WHY (purpose, goals), where you add the most value and what is most important to you?

- **STOP** – what are you going to stop doing that adds no value to your WHY. It may have added value at some point in time, now it is creating a roadblock.

- **START** – to identify 1-3 core areas of focus at any one time. It could be adapting new behaviours, habits, and skills in the next 90 days to get you to your WHY.

- **SHARE** – your plan with a mentor, coach, buddy, or someone you respect who is knowledgeable in these areas and with whom you can check in on your progress – what's working and areas of focus. Share your wins and failures openly without feeling judged.

- **ACCOUNTABILITY** – No matter what is working and not working, you are accountable for the decisions, behaviours, and direction choices you make. Life does not go perfectly to plan so we all need to learn and adjust as we go. Empower yourself to be accountable and to learn valuable lessons along your journey. Stay in touch with me and feel free to share your journey as you apply your key learnings. You can reach me via the following.

LinkedIn	www.linkedin.com/in/vannessa-mccamley
Facebook	www.facebook.com/vannessamccamleylinksuccess
Website	www.linksuccess.com.au/rewire-for-success

References and Resources

Books and articles

Dancing research references:

Edwards, S. (2015). *Dancing and the brain.* Harvard Medical School. Coventry University. (2018). *Salsa Dancing Boosts Brain Function.* **Retrieved from** www.coventry.ac.uk/primary-news/salsa-dancing-boosts-brain-function-says-coventry-university-study-for-tv-show article

Laguipo, A. (2019) *Is Dancing Good for the Brain.* New Medical Life Sciences. **Retrieved from** www.news-medical.net/health/Is-Dancing-Good-for-the-Brain.aspx

Verghese, J. (2003). *Leisure Activities and the Risk of Dementia in the Elderly* New England Journal of Medicine. **Retrieved from** www.nejm.org/doi/full/10.1056/NEJMoa022252

Merom, D., Grunseit, A., Erammudugolla, R., Jefferis, B., Mcneill, J., Anstey, K. (2016). *Cognitive Benefits of Social Dancing and Walking in Old Age: The Dancing Mind Randomized Controlled Trial.* Frontiers in Aging Neuroscience. **Retrieved from** www.frontiersin.org/articles/10.3389/fnagi.2016.00026

Machattie, E. (2015) *How Playing Music Benefits your Brain More than Any Other Activity.* www.merriammusic.com/school-of-music/music-brain-activity

Other

Berkman, L. F., & Syme, S. L. (1979). *Social networks, host resistance, and mortality: A nine year follow up study of Alameda County residents.* American Journal of Epidemiology, 109, 186–204.

Brown, B. (2018). *Dare to Lead: Brave Work. Tough Conversations. Whole hearts.* Random House. London.

Cigna & Ipsos (2018). *Cigna U.S. loneliness index: Survey of 20,000 Americans examining behaviors driving loneliness in the United States.* Cigna. Bloomfield.

Czyz, E. K., Liu, Z. & King, C. A. (2012). *Social Connectedness and One-Year Trajectories among Suicidal Adolescents Following Psychiatric Hospitalization.* J Clin Child Adolesc Psychol.; 41(2): 214–226.

Fanning, J. R. & Pietrzakab, R. H. (2013). *Suicidality among older male veterans in the United States: Results from the National Health and Resilience in Veterans Study.* Journal of Psychiatric Research, 47(11), 1766-1775.

Hall & Partners Open Mind and Beyondblue (2014). *Men's Social Connectedness.* **Retrieved from** www.beyondblue.org.au/docs/default-source/research-project-files/bw0276-mens-social-connectedness-final.pdf?

Halber, D. (2018). Motivation: Why you Do the things You Do. **Retrieved from** www.brainfacts.org/thinking-sensing-and-behaving/learning-and-memory/2018/motivation-why-you-do-the-things-you-do-082818

Holt-Lunstad, J., Smith, T.B. & Layton, J.B. (2010) *Social Relationships and Mortality Risk: A Meta-analytic Review.* PLoS Medicine 7(7): e1000316. doi:10.1371/ journal.pmed.1000316.

Kahneman, D. (2011) *Thinking Fast and Slow.* Doubleday. Toronto.

Kim D.A., Benjamin E.J., Fowler, J.H. & Christakis, N.A. (2016). *Social connectedness is associated with fibrinogen level in a human social network.* Proc. R. Soc. B 283: 20160958.

Kintzle, S., Barr, N., Corletto, G. & Castro, C.A (2018). *PTSD in U.S. Veterans: The Role of Social Connectedness, Combat Experience and Discharge.* Healthcare, 6, 102.

Lancee, B., & Radl, J. (2012). *Social connectedness and the transition from work to retirement.* The Journals of Gerontology, Series B: Psychological Sciences and Social Sciences, 67(4), 481–490.

Lieberman, M., Eisenberger, N. (2009). *Pains and Pleasures of Social Life* Science magazine. www.science.sciencemag.org/content/323/5916/890/tab-figures-data

McGonigal, K. (2015). *The Upside of Stress.* Avery Publishing Group. New York.

Mackay, S. (2020). *Fear of the Unknown. 7 Strategies to Build a Resilient Brain in Uncertain Times* **Retrieved from** www.linkedin.com/pulse/fear-unknown-7-strategies-build-resilient-brain-uncertain-sarah-mckay

Reyes, M. E. S., Davis, R. D., Chua, C. A. P. Q., Olaveria, G. L., Pamintuan, L. J. E., et al. (2020). *Relative Importance of Social Support and Social Connectedness as Protective Factors of Suicidal Ideation Among Selected Filipino Late Adolescents.* Suicidology Online; 11(1), 29-40.

Smith, B.J. & Lim, M.H. (2020). *How the COVID-19 pandemic is focusing attention on loneliness and social isolation.* Public Health Res Pract. 2020;30(2): e3022008.

Stegemoller. E. (2017) *Exploring the Mechanisms of Music Therapy.* The Scientist www.the-scientist.com/features/exploring-the-mechanisms-of-music-therapy-31936

Sugisawa, H., Liang, J., & Liu, X. (1994). *Social networks, social support, and mortality among older people in Japan.* Journal of Gerontology, 49(1), S3–S13.

The National Centre for Biotechnology Information advances science and health by providing access to biomedical and genomic information. Social Cognitive and affective Neuroscience research. In the article, *Grit and the brain: spontaneous activity of the dorsomedial prefrontal cortex mediates the relationship between the trait grit and academic performance* it talks about 'grit' as a personality trait and its importance for achieving long-term goals. Broadly, grit is a subcomponent of the complex construct of self-regulation (McClelland et al., 2015), and mounting empirical evidence has indicated that the PFC (Pre-frontal Cortex) is closely associated with self-regulation (Kelley et al., 2015). The findings suggest that the PFC, which is related to goal-directed thought and behavior (Fuster, 1988; Stuss and Knight, 2013), task management and planning (Koechlin et al., 2000; Tanji et al., 2007), and cognitive control (Miller and Cohen, 2001; Ridderinkhof et al., 2004; Taren et al., 2011), may play an essential role in individual differences in grit. www.ncbi.nlm.nih.gov/pmc/articles/PMC5390743

Oxford Academic, Social Cognitive and Affective Neuroscience Journal (self-affirmation), Matthew D. Lieberman Christopher N. Cascio, Matthew Brook O'Donnell, Francis J. Tinney, Shelley E. Taylor, Victor J. Strecher, Emily B. Falk (2015) www.academic.oup.com/scan/article/11/4/621/2375054?login=true

Myth – You can't teach an old dog new tricks – article links that supports this statement:
www.neurosciencenews.com/learning-mechanism-adult-brain-inhibitory-synapses 2012

www.neurosciencenews.com/aging-thinking-learning-reasoning-5434 2016

www.inside-the-brain.com/2018/07/29/rewiring-the-brain-teaching-an-old-dog-new-tricks 2018

Videos

Brown, B. (2010). *The Power of Vulnerability*. www.ted.com/talks/brene_brown_the_power_of_vulnerability/transcript?language=en (20:03 min) TEDx Houston

Collins, A. (2014). *How Playing an Instrument Benefits your Brain* youtu.be/R0JKCYZ8hng (4:44 mins)
This is a great TED Ed presentation on the benefits of learning a musical instrument.

Lieberman, M., Eisenberger, N. (2010) *Social Pain and Physical Pain*. www.youtube.com/watch?v=X7EFYwUopf8 (4:38 mins)
Dr Matthew Lieberman and Dr Naomi Eisenberger (husband and wife team) have been interested in social pain and have undertaken interesting research that shows that some of the same neural regions that we see active when we experience physical pain are also active when we experience social pain.

McGonigal, K. (2015). B*elieve it or Not, Stress Can be Good For You.*
www.youtube.com/watch?v=IaVKXx767rw (3:34 mins)
Kelly McGonigal is a health psychologist and lecturer at Stanford University who is known for her work in the field of 'science help' which focuses on translating insights from psychology and neuroscience into practical strategies that support health and well-being.

Siegal, D. (2012). *Hand Model of the Brain*
www.youtube.com/watch?v=gm9ClJ74Oxwon (2:31 mins).
Siegal is Clinical Professor of Psychiatry, author of several books and Director of the Mindsight Institute. He has a really simple way of explaining the brain. It is so simple you can share it with children but it's also really effective in sharing with adults to explain the relationship between our emotional and our rational brain.

Simon Sinek (2017) START WITH WHY – The golden circle video: www.youtube.com/watch?v=i-89IO5M7Lc (5:55 mins)

SENTIS. (2012). *Neuroplasticity.* www.youtube.com/watch?v=ELpfYCZa87g (2 mins)
This is a brilliant 2 min video to explain through animation on how it works.

Neuroscience of leadership programme certifications

Thank you to the following programme's that have provided valuable knowledge and insights that I have shared in this book to make a difference in the lives of others.

Advance Diploma of Neuroscience of Leadership, Neurocapability
Linda Ray is the CEO of NeuroCapability.
www.neurocapability.com.au

Accredited NeuroTREAD™ facilitator of EnHansen Performance.
Kristen Hansen is the founder of EnHansen Performance, a leadership and performance consulting business and author of the book TRACTION.
www.enhansenperformance.com.au

Certified practitioner, PRISM Brain Mapping – Behavioural profiling
Tiffany Gray is the Director of PRISM Brain Mapping in Australia.
www.prismbrainmapping.com

Sites for professional help

General

Beyond Blue website for information and help with depression and anxiety: www.beyondblue.org.au and phone number 1300 22 4636 within Australia.

American Institute of Stress www.stress.org

Where to get professional sleep help

To see a sleep specialist or sleep psychologist you require a referral from your GP. Online programs can usually be self-referred. Here are some separate links for pediatric and adult professional help both online and clinic settings.

Lisa Maltman is Founder of The Sleep Connection. If you are interest in running a Corporate, Community or School Program, then please contact her via lisa@thesleepconnection.com.au For more information, resources and videos for children and teens www.thesleepconnection.com.au/

American Academy of Sleep Medicine www.sleepeducation.org/news/2013/08/01/sleep-and-caffeine

Sleep Shack – an online program for sleep problems in pre-teens and teens www.sleepshack.com.au

Sleepio – An online program tailored for adults, to help improve poor sleep. **Sleepio-Expert articles & guides are highly recommended reading.**

Woolcock Paediatric Sleep Clinic – Australia's specialist Paediatric and Adolescent Sleep Service which assesses and manages all sleep disorders in children and teenagers. The team includes sleep specialists, psychologists, psychiatrists, and ENT's. www.woolcock.org.au/our-clinical-services/paediatric-sleep-clinic

Woolcock Adult Sleep Clinic – A world-leading medical centre, based in Glebe, specialising in the diagnosis and treatment of all sleep and breathing disorders. www.woolcock.org.au/our-clinical-services/sleep-study

The Sleep Health Foundation – Australia's Leading Advocate for Healthy Sleep, with information on most sleep topics www.sleephealthfoundation.org.au/fact-sheets.html

Sites for contributors and techniques

Kerrin Booth graduated as a Naturopath in 1992 and has her practice focused on nutrition, herbal medicine and Australian Bush Flower Essences to help a wide variety of health problems www.kerrinboothnaturopath.com

Dr Delia McCabe – Neuroscientist focused on neurobiology of stress and nutrition www.lighterbrighteryou.life

Dr Craig Duncan – Sports Performance Scientists www.drcraigduncan.com.au

Daniel Garbett – Breathwork specialist and app www.feel-alive.com.au/breathwork

Nivriti Gargya – Yoga therapist, Pranic Healer, Founder and Senior Teacher, Mystique Moksha Yoga Studio www.mystiquemoksha.com.au

Nicole Masseque – Music therapies www.facebook.com/utchenge

Dr Joe Dispenza – Neuroscientist and author www.drjoedispenza.com and newsletter on the topic of 'Emotions are not your enemy'

Lynne Goldberg – Co-founder Breethe mindfulness and sleep app www.breethe.com

Francesco Cirillo – For brain breaks. He created a time management technique developed in the late 1980s www.todoist.com/productivity-methods/pomodoro-technique Here is a timer set up to use; www.pomofocus.io

www.ingramcontent.com/pod-product-compliance
Lightning Source LLC
Chambersburg PA
CBHW051436290426
44109CB00016B/1582